STUDIES IN FRENCH LITERATURE No. 29

*General Editor*
W. G. Moore
Emeritus Fellow of St John's College, Oxford

# EMILE ZOLA:
# GERMINAL

by

COLIN SMETHURST
*Lecturer in French, University of Liverpool*

EDWARD ARNOLD

First published 1974
by Edward Arnold (Publishers) Ltd
25 Hill Street, London W1X 8LL

Cloth edition ISBN: 0 7131 5772 0
Paper edition ISBN: 0 7131 5773 9

*Printed in Great Britain by*
*The Camelot Press Ltd, Southampton*

# *Contents*

# *Acknowledgements*

The edition of *Germinal* to which reference is made in this book is Le Livre de poche (1964). The publishers' thanks are due to Editeurs Fasquelle, Paris, for permission to reproduce copyright material from this edition.

# 1. Background

Until about twenty years ago Zola was rarely regarded as worthy of 'serious' study. The novels were read, indeed widely read, as a sort of relaxation literature, and to confess to liking them was much like confessing to a passion for horror films or a taste for jelly babies, just a little this side of guilt or vulgarity, and in any case not too important one way or the other. For some, however, Zola's name lived not for his novels, but essentially in connection with the Dreyfus affair, his famous article *J'Accuse* having played an important role in helping to reopen the trial of the Army officer whose unjust condemnation was the centre of a vast political storm at the turn of the century. Here, the appreciation of Zola was essentially non-literary, an expression, rather, of admiration for the champion of notions of justice and truth.

If judgments on the literary value of Zola's novels were made, they were usually little more than distant echoes of the great quarrels that thundered around him in his life-time. Unhealthy, obscene, pornographic were the commonly-invoked epithets of the anti-Zola brigade. It is significant that Clement K. Shorter's article in the *Sphere* (23 October 1915) quoted in the court case which resulted in the banning of D. H. Lawrence's *The Rainbow* should link the name of these two 'shocking' writers. Shorter claims:

> Zola's novels are child's food compared with the strong meat contained in . . . *The Rainbow*.

For a certain sort of reader Lawrence produced the same sense of shock as did Zola forty or so years before. Such an attitude does not get the literary critic very far, but does at least testify to the power of Zola to hit hard. It is connected, too, with the idea that some subjects and some ways of treating them are not fit for literature. Sex and the working class tended to be taboo for the type of aesthete interested in disembodied study of passion and the soul. Although such an attitude is relatively rare nowadays, and indeed the reverse often seems the more conventional view, it still persists implicitly in many ways. For example, in one of the standard manuals for teaching French literature in French schools today, edited by Lagarde and Michard, the volume on French nineteenth-century literature devotes five or six times less space to Zola than to Chateaubriand or Lamartine, and tends to talk more about his Naturalist theories of literature than about his actual literary achievement.

The theories of Naturalism which Zola propounded provided in the past the basis for a more subtle way of hitting at the novelist. To some extent Zola brought this on himself by his persistent championing in works like *Le Roman expérimental* of the cause of Naturalism in literature and his repeated claims that he wrote his novels according to such theories. Basically, he was attempting to adapt some of the principles of mid-nineteenth-century scientific thought for use in writing novels, hence his insistence on the science of heredity and the experimental method. With this he combined a certain positivist materialism. He claimed that the result, in spite of the inevitable hesitations any pioneer must feel, was more logical, more true, than the great but, for Zola, too intuitive realism of a Balzac. These theories were criticized on the grounds that a novelist cannot be in the same position as an experimental scientist. Although the novelist may to some extent be able to proceed 'scientifically' from a hypothesis about human conduct in society to the setting up of an 'experiment' to test the hypothesis (i.e. situate a certain sort of character in a specific environment, then introduce an event), he cannot then stand back and observe the results of his experiment, for he is intervening at every stage, in every word he writes on the page.

Zola, then, was attacked on one flank for producing a theory of the novel which was philosophically unsound, and in any case inadequate aesthetically, and on another flank by those who, accepting the theory, showed his documentation to be insufficient or distorted. Disgust at what was held to be sordid or obscene in his works and/or complaints of intellectual inadequacy were the two major themes taken up by the detractors of Zola.

The opposing view of Zola's work was usually put by insisting that his writing was powerful, vivid, and incorporated a great sense of poetry. The poetic vision was seen as sometimes lyrical, but more often epic in its quality. These epic aspects in his novels had been strongly stressed by Jules Lemaître in a long critical appreciation in *La Revue politique et littéraire* of 14 March 1885 (re-published in *Les Contemporains*, 1ère série). It was often variations on the article of Lemaître which provided the staple positive view of Zola until relatively recently, and the article itself is still worthwhile reading.

Lemaître's review was written on the occasion of the publication of *Germinal*, and was an attempt to give a complete view of the work of Zola up to that moment in time, a moment which we can now see as being just over half-way through the author's literary career. Lemaître eliminates from the discussion Zola's theories of literature and denounces those critics who, having discovered that the novels do not follow the theories of Naturalism claim, therefore, that Zola is a poor novelist. He quite rightly concentrates on a study of the novels themselves, and insists on the genius of Zola in conveying a sense of great drama, vast masses observed and set in motion, a swarming and limitless vision:

> Je ne sache pas que dans aucun roman on ait fait vivre ni remué de pareilles masses. . . . Le poète déroule avec sa patience robuste, avec sa brutalité morne, avec sa largeur d'évocation, une série de vastes et lamentables tableaux, composés de détails monochromes qui s'entassent, s'entassent, montent et s'étalent comme une marée. . . .

This piling up of detail on detail contributes to the sense of inevitability in his works. Everything takes place under the sign of fatality. Fate, for Zola, is not the feeling of random and cruel acts of the gods ruling Nature such as one finds in Hardy's novels, but the purposeful series of ultimately creative acts controlling human destiny.

> M. Zola [Lemaître continues] a magnifiquement rendu ce qu'il y a de fatál, d'aveugle, d'impersonnel, d'irrésistible dans un drame de cette sorte, la contagion des colères rassemblées, l'âme collective des foules. . . . N'avais-je pas raison d'appeler M. Zola un poète épique? et les caractères dominants de ses longs récits ne sont-ce pas précisément ceux de l'épopée?

Nobody nowadays denies the vast canvases, the feeling for the surging of masses in movement, a huge and powerful epic vision in Zola's works. Unfortunately this appreciation came to be used by critics to express virtually the whole of Zola's genius. Sometimes this epic quality, while being grudgingly accorded, was used to deny any other aspects of interest in his works. It is hoped that the following pages may suggest some further possible ways of reading Zola.

## The Rougon-Macquart series

*Germinal* was published as a serial in the newspaper *Gil Blas* from 26 November 1884 to 25 February 1885, and soon after in book form. It is the thirteenth novel of twenty which appeared between 1870 and 1893 under the generic title *Les Rougon-Macquart: histoire naturelle et sociale d'une famille sous le Second Empire*. This vast series of novels by no means exhausts the catalogue of Zola's literary production, indeed represents rather less than half of what was published in volume form in his lifetime, to which one must add the huge number of his journalistic writings which remained uncollected at the time of his death. In spite of the unity in the Rougon-Macquart series and its central position in Zola's writings, a good deal of recent critical examination[1] has shown that there is no complete break between these twenty novels and his other works, but on the contrary a great deal of continuity of subject matter and treatment between the early works (1865–70), the late works (1894–1902) and the central massif of the Rougon-Macquart novels.

While bearing in mind such conclusions, let us examine what is at least a unity of intention in the Rougon-Macquart series. The original idea was for a series of ten novels, and arose in Zola's mind in late 1868. Several sets of notes[2] dating from 1868–9 show Zola working out for himself in general terms the subjects of these novels and analysing their theoretical basis, or what he calls 'la carcasse intime'. A good proportion of these notes contains references to, and summaries of, works on physiology. There is the beginning of an adaptation of them for use in the novels with particular emphasis being laid on hereditary influences on human beings. Although many of the 'laws' of heredity quoted by Zola are now discredited, they do at least provide him with a system of references, a partial framework. They also have the advantage of being fairly flexible, thus giving Zola the liberty of ignoring them if he wishes. This can be done by falling back, for example, on the law of 'innéité', which allows that new individuals may be created whose characteristics do not depend on inherited factors. Such major characters as Pascal Rougon (*Le Docteur Pascal*) and Jean Macquart (*La Terre; La Débâcle*) are examples of Zola's use of the 'innéité' principle. Zola was certainly aware of the vagueness and hesitations in this relatively new science, but was nevertheless willing to use it as an aid in structuring the at first sight enormous variety and terrifying anarchy of Nature. It is present in these early notes, used in varying degrees in all the novels,

[1] For example: John C. Lapp, *Zola before the Rougon-Macquart* (University of Toronto Press, 1964); F. W. J. Hemmings, 'Les sources d'inspiration de Zola conteur', *Cahiers naturalistes* 24–5 (1963), 29–44.

[2] Reproduced in Zola, *Les Rougon-Macquart* (Pléiade), vol. V, 1674–1781, from which the unattributed quotations in this section are taken.

and re-stated very fully in the final novel of the series, *Le Docteur Pascal*. Its presence is given pictorial form in the family tree of the Rougon-Macquarts, which Zola first sketched out in 1869, then published with modifications and additions in 1878, and whose final version appeared at the front of *Le Docteur Pascal* in 1893. We shall see the usefulness of the heredity factor when we come to a detailed study of Etienne Lantier.

Associated with these early notes on human, and indeed animal, physiology are some remarks which are concerned with establishing a sort of primitive sociology. They have less theoretical and scientific backing than the notes on heredity, but appear to fulfil the same function for Zola of reducing the chaos of life to some semblance of order. Humanity is divided into social groupings, called 'mondes' by Zola. He hesitates as to whether there should be three or four groups, decides on the latter and classifies them as 'Peuple, Commerçants, Bourgeoisie, Grand Monde', then finally tacks on a 'monde à part' which must rank as one of the most bizarre social categories ever invented, including as it does prostitute, murderer, priest and artist. The groups are formed as groups by the influence of 'milieu', both physical and social ('milieu de lieu et milieu de société'). There is an element of circularity in this argument—social groups are formed by the social group in which they live—but the result in the novels is one of concentration of effect, often of claustrophobia, or of an inability to escape from the influence of environment.

At this point Zola encounters the problem of having had an illustrious predecessor working in the same field—Balzac. Balzac, too, had created a unity out of a series of separate works and published them under the generic title of *La Comédie humaine*. He, too, had developed a detailed and comprehensive system of social categories, and had tried to provide an overall picture of society and its influence on the individual. Zola reacts by determining to concentrate his efforts on the study of one family, and by subordinating the social study to the scientific. As a final difference, Zola depicts Balzac as writing in the light of his political and religious persuasions and prejudices, whereas he, Zola, wishes to approach his subject impartially, scientifically: 'Je me contenterai d'être savant, de dire ce qui est . . .'. Zola might have tried aligning this statement with Balzac's in his preface to the *Comédie humaine*: 'La société française allait être l'historien, je ne devais être que le secrétaire.' There is certainly less of a distinction here between the two authors' theories than Zola is willing to admit or accept, and so he falls back on his argument of the increased scientific value of his own work, and, as a minor point, on the fact that he is dealing with the society of the Second Empire and not of the Restauration and July Monarchy as Balzac was. In any case, Zola says, 'Si j'accepte un cadre historique, c'est uniquement pour avoir un milieu qui réagisse.'

This statement protests too much, and certainly when Zola submits an outline plan to his publisher Lacroix in 1869, he is writing equally categorically that the series will be based on two ideas:

1° Etudier dans une famille les questions de sang et de milieux . . .
2° Etudier tout le Second Empire, depuis le coup d'Etat jusqu'à nos jours.

By the time Zola had finished *La Curée*, the second novel of the series, the Second Empire had already collapsed in ruins and Zola found himself left as historian of a period now complete in itself and covering the years 1851–71.

Declarations of intent, like political manifestos, are used to concentrate thought and give it direction. This basically is what Zola is doing in all these meditations before launching himself into his series. His intent, again like political manifestos, is often transformed by circumstances. All things considered, however, Zola remains remarkably close to the task he set himself in 1868–9, which he summarized in his plan sent to Lacroix. He keeps returning to it after seeming to ignore it or play it down in some of his novels, until it reaches its apotheosis in *Le Docteur Pascal* written over twenty years later.

Some of the parts of this philosophical backbone to *Les Rougon-Macquart* seem to have been hit on almost by chance, and are adopted simply for functional reasons. Zola's tone and attitudes emerge clearly in the following remarks he makes on materialism as a philosophy:

Prendre avant tout une tendance philosophique, non pour l'étaler, mais pour donner une unité à mes livres. La meilleure serait peut-être le matérialisme, je veux dire la croyance en des forces sur lesquelles je n'aurai jamais besoin de m'expliquer. Le mot force ne compromet pas. Mais il ne faut plus user du mot fatalité qui serait ridicule dans dix volumes. Le fatalisme est un vieil outil.

One can see the way Zola is snatching at ideas which are in the air fashionable even, in the 1860s, and using them as convenient props substituting force for fatality simply because the latter smells old-fashioned.

Relatively little of this ideological casting around and exploring of, possibilities is connected with the art of the novelist as such. The few remarks Zola does make on this subject, however, suggest a Zola with whom the readers of his works will feel immediately familiar:

> Ne pas oublier qu'un drame prend le public à la gorge. Il se fâche, mais n'oublie pas. Lui donner toujours, sinon des cauchemars, du moins des livres excessifs qui restent dans sa mémoire . . . toujours de la chaleur et de la passion. Un torrent grondant, mais large, et d'une marche majestueuse.

This is the vocabulary and technique of Zola's major works.

Behind the props of mid-nineteenth-century scientific thought and the attempts at careful distinguishing of his novels from those of Balzac, we can see at work a view of the world that is essentially biological in its arguments, attempting to analyse the relative importance of nature and nurture and the relationship between them.

## A novel about the working class

Part of the fame of Zola has been based on his reputation as the novelist of the working class, be it the peasantry or the industrial proletariat. What is surprising is that this aspect of his work developed relatively slowly and filled only a small role in the initial plans for the Rougon-Macquart series. In Zola's original list of ten subjects, only one is designated 'Un roman ouvrier (Paris)', although it is true that Zola also intended to write 'Un roman militaire (Italie)'—i.e. a novel on the Italian war of 1859—and had included the soldier among his social category 'Peuple'. A later version of this plan for ten novels elaborates on the subject of the 'roman ouvrier':

> Peinture d'un ménage d'ouvriers à notre époque. Drame intime et profond de la déchéance du travailleur parisien sous la déplorable influence du milieu des barrières et des cabarets.

This is quite clearly the outline of the novel which is to become *L'Assommoir*, the seventh novel in the Rougon-Macquart series, and contains little or nothing in common with *Germinal*.

A list of novels drawn up in 1871 or 1872 shows that the series has now swollen to seventeen. Only two are designated as novels on the working class, the first still clearly the future *L'Assommoir*, the second:

Un 2<sup>e</sup> roman ouvrier.—Particulièrement politique. L'ouvrier de l'insurrection, outil révolutionnaire, de la Commune. Une photographie d'insurgé tué en 48. Aboutissant à mai 71.

In addition, the 'roman militaire (Italie)' has now been diversified in location and split into two: 'Le roman sur la guerre d'Italie', and the 'Roman sur [la guerre] le siège et la Commune'. In other words, a major transformation in the series has occurred as a result of the Franco-Prussian war of 1870–71, the ensuing collapse of Napoleon III's Empire and the Paris Commune of March–May 1871. The latter half of the series is now to contain three novels centred on these episodes and serves as a good example of how Zola, in spite of his intentions of furnishing an overall portrait of the Second Empire, has in fact crowded the bulk of his novels towards the latter part of the period, where his emphasis on the frenetic, the degenerate and the catastrophic can have fullest play.

The intended novel on the political role of the working class during the Commune is one result of these events. In the end, of course, no one novel is devoted entirely to this subject, and the topic is used only to provide an apocalyptic ending to *La Débâcle*, the novel of the Franco-Prussian war and its aftermath, which came to replace the earlier project of the military novel on the Italian war of 1859. What is even more significant is that the major figure in Zola's account of the events of the Commune is a neurotic bourgeois intellectual, and not at all a representative of the working class. One *communard*, Chouteau, is a member of the working class, but his role in the Commune is shown as criminal rather than political, and his part in the novel is only minor. In any case, *La Débâcle* was the penultimate novel of the series and was written and published seven years after *Germinal*. Thus, although the Franco-Prussian war and the Commune directed Zola's attention quite firmly to the political role of the working class, the subject is not taken up in the short term.

*L'Assommoir* (1876–7) was the first novel which Zola devoted entirely to the study of the working class. Its publication gave rise to strong criticism, not only from middle-class critics on grounds of taste and morality, but also from representatives of working-class movements for its political ambiguity. Zola was accused of attacking the workers for their alcoholism and moral degradation. The socialist Charles Floquet denounced in 1879:

le calomniateur public par son œuvre malsaine et ordurière, cet

auteur d'un pamphlet ridicule dirigé contre les travailleurs et forgeant
ainsi des armes pour la réaction.[3]

These criticisms from diverse sources are, in their way, a tribute to
Zola's naturalist aesthetic, and notably his attempts to provide a description of a situation without including either an overt moral or an overt
political attitude on the part of the author. Floquet's remarks cannot
stand as fair criticism for there is in *L'Assommoir* an implicit morality of
pity and charity in the face of such misery. It is, however, also certain
that Zola underplays in this novel the political role of the working class,
driving it into the margin of the work. He claimed that this was his
intention, and that the political aspects would be dealt with later in
another novel:

> J'indique au dénouement le vaste mouvement de réunions publiques
> qui se prépare. Plus tard, dans un roman, j'étudierai ce moment
> curieux d'une façon complète; le roman de Gervaise [i.e. *L'Assommoir*]
> n'est pas le roman politique.[4]

At the time of the publication of *L'Assommoir* Zola is still not envisag-
ing a novel on a strike situation, or on the mining industry. His intentions
are still to write a novel on the Parisian worker and the Commune.
*Germinal*, startid seven years later, is evidence that a whole series of
influences in the intervening period have culminated in the desire to
tackle head-on what was then called 'la question sociale', the 'problem'
of the working class, and to deal with in in a typical and enduring
situation rather than the extraordinary and temporary situation of the
Commune. The novel retains nevertheless some of the attitudes of
fright and pity which for Zola had first crystallized round his experience
of the Paris Commune. Indeed *Germinal* can be seen as Zola's novel on
the Commune transposed into a more everyday register.

### The function of documentation

Documentation plays, of course, an important part in Zola's conception of his role as a scientific novelist. In his critical study *Le Roman
expérimental* Zola indicates it as the raw material on which the novelist

[3] Quoted by A. Lanoux in his Preface to Zola, *Les Rougon-Macquart*
(Pléiade), vol. I, xxxiv.

[4] *Ebauche* of *L'Assommoir*: Bibliothèque nationale MS., n.a.f. 10345,
f. 129.

starts to carry out his experiments. It always formed part of the public stance of the naturalist novelist, and Zola was still declaring his faithfulness to it as a method even after completing the Rougon-Macquart series.

The term document is used broadly by Zola to mean both written sources and personal observation or inquiry. In the case of *Germinal* the written sources range from medical studies on illnesses in the mining industry to histories of socialism and newspaper clippings on strikes and court cases arising from them; the personal observation comes from a visit to Anzin in 1884 and is transcribed in the dossier which Zola entitled *Mes Notes sur Anzin*.

There is absolutely no doubt that Zola did provide himself with 'documents' in the course of preparing each of his novels. The difficulty is in establishing exactly at what stage they intervene in the composition of the work and hence what importance they have in the creative process. It is highly doubtful that they form simply an external and objective starting-point as Zola would often have us believe. Close study of the preparatory dossiers for the novels has led many recent commentators, reacting against the views propagated by Zola himself and by early students of his works, to place higher value on imaginative intuition than on documentation. A more satisfying solution, and the one that comes nearest to the facts of the composition of *Germinal*, is to see the novel as resulting from a fruitful interpenetration of the two, the one testing, influencing, transforming or eliminating the other. This is the conclusion which Richard H. Zakarian has reached after a study of some of the sources of *Germinal*, that the 'imaginative and documentary processes are totally interdependent and concurrent, that is to say, that in some cases imagination dictates the selection of certain facts and in others the document may suggest a highly dramatic incident which, ironically founded in truth, may seem much too incredible to be believable, and thus must either be discarded or modified before use'.[5]

If this explains satisfactorily the relations between documentation and imagination, it hardly shows the exact function of documentation in Zola's view of the world. In general terms, it derives from his materialism and from the emphasis placed by writers in the realist tradition on the importance of the physical reality surrounding human beings. But

[5] Richard H. Zakarian, *Zola's 'Germinal': A Critical Study of its Primary Sources* (Droz, 1972), 4; see also H. Mitterand, 'Quelques aspects de la création littéraire dans l'œuvre d'Emile Zola', *Cahiers naturalistes* 24–5 (1963), 9–20.

Flaubert and the Goncourt brothers, too, insisted on documentation, and yet its function in their novels is not the one we find in Zola's novels. A scene which may be interpreted as encapsulating Zola's view is that of Pauline Quenu's first menstruation in *La Joie de vivre*,[6] the novel which precedes *Germinal* in the Rougon-Macquart series. The young orphan girl is not prepared for this moment by her guardian and her first reaction is one of mixed horror, fascination and the conviction that she is going to die, all translated by Zola into hectic language. As the fever caused by her experience subsides she then applies herself to the systematic study of the *Traité de physiologie* by Longuet and the *Anatomie descriptive* by Cruveilhier. She examines particularly closely the illustrative plates of the anatomy volume, 'es planches superbes d'une réalité saignante', and arrives at a serious, dignified understanding and acceptance of the functions of the body. Zola's own neurotic horrors and fears, particularly those concerned with body functions, are similarly brought under control by his 'scientific' method, his use of documentation. The final picture is still of a 'réalité saignante', but instead of overwhelming the observer it has now been brought into focus and understood, and serves to testify to the enduring qualities of life. The notion that Zola's documentation is simply a sort of journalistic reportage slipped into his works is inadequate.

## Preparatory work on Germinal

First, a distinction between preparations made deliberately with the idea of a novel on a strike in a mining community in mind, and the more diffuse influences on Zola himself occurring over a much longer period of time which gradually turn him towards such a subject. The former, thanks to the working methods of Zola and his habit of preserving the notes, plans and sketches which result from them, are fairly well known even though they need delicate interpretation to be fully understood. In the case of *Germinal* these preparations cover the first three months of 1884 and immediately precede the composition of the work itself. The earlier, more diffuse influences have to be inferred from the known facts of Zola's life and the social history of the period through which he lived. They concern the largely passive, even unconscious, acquisition of experience which goes to the formation of attitudes. In

[6] Zola, *Les Rougon-Macquart* (Pléiade), vol. III, 852–4.

relation to the composition of a given novel, this stage has been designated by Henri Mitterand as a period of 'pré-maturation':

> une documentation primitive, non dirigée, qui précède . . . la documentation directe et spécialisée . . . et qui n'est pas la moins importante, bien que ses traces n'apparaissent presque jamais dans les dossiers préparatoires.[7]

We have already mentioned the Commune for the important, even traumatic effects it had on Zola's approach to the political problems posed to the bourgeois state by the working class. Other influences go back further still, and relate to events under the Second Empire, notably to the sequence of strikes in the France of the 1860s.

Evidence of varying weight has been produced suggesting that Zola was familar with a long series of strikes in most of the mining areas of France from 1861 through to 1884, and that echoes from several of them sound through the pages of Germinal. Much of the topography of the novel points to Montsou being based on Anzin and partially on Denain, near Valenciennes, a few kilometres from the Belgian border. Zola visited Anzin and took copious notes during the course of a long strike there in 1884, at the very period when he was composing the sketch for Germinal. This visit is thus part of the conscious documentation. However, this was by no means the first strike there, and it has been suggested[8] Zola may also have had in mind a strike at Anzin which had occurred in 1866, the precise date of the strike in Germinal. Zola's dossiers for the novel refer clearly to other strikes at La Ricamarie, Aubin, Le Creusot and Montceau-les-Mines, which had taken place at various dates before and after the collapse of the Second Empire.

A very large number of strikes had occurred in 1869 and 1870, producing a public opinion aware of and sensitive to the new dimensions given to this sort of industrial action. The phenomenon was not limited to France; a similar atmosphere in Britain in the 1860s resulted in the publication of the report of the *Royal Commission on the Organization and Rules of Trade Unions and other Associations* (1867-9). This strike-sensitive social atmosphere that was one of the preliminaries to the downfall of the Empire is used by Zola, even though he may have pushed the events to a date a year or two earlier in time than was actually the case. They remain nevertheless highly plausible. Zola is deliberately

[7] H. Mitterand, *art. cit.*, 13-14.

[8] Henri Marel, 'Une source possible de Germinal?', *Cahiers naturalistes* 39 (1970), 49-60.

vague about the exact dating of the events of his novel, stretching the time-scale as he does to suit his dramatic purposes, and in any case one might argue from another angle that *Germinal* is very exactly situated in time and reflects the economic slump of 1866-7. Such arguments become trivial when one realizes that the general impression of a strike taking place some time in the 1860s is satisfactorily conveyed. Moreover, a strike situation, while varying in detail from strike to strike, has a fairly consistent structure. Even such a towering genius as Eisenstein follows a pattern in his film *Strike* (1924) which, while describing a strike in Tsarist Russia, is remarkably similar to Zola's *Germinal*: the presentation of normal life in a factory, an immediate issue causing the strike, the factory lying idle, the effects of a prolonged strike on the workers, a massacre engineered, repression and its effects.

One might assume that another aspect of the undirected and passive assimilation of the background to his novel is in the politics of the various working-class movements. Here, however, Zola is relatively uninformed until he begins the active preparation of the novel, and there are grounds for thinking that *Germinal* serves as the story of the education in working-class politics not only of Etienne Lantier, but also of Zola himself. One can see some of the distance covered in the transition from the largely a-political description of artisans in *L'Assommoir* written in 1877 to the highly political description of class consciousness among the industrial proletariat in *Germinal* written in 1884-5. Nevertheless, Zola was not unaware of political developments in France in the 1860s, mainly through his journalistic contacts. His articles in the progressive newspapers *La Tribune* and *La Cloche* in the year or two before the collapse of the Empire show a Zola denouncing indignantly the ruling bourgeoisie, and reporting Parliamentary debates, among them discussions on the role of the International Working Men's Association.

When we come closer to the date of composition of *Germinal* the information about Zola's documentation is much richer, and has been much studied.[9] Zola seems to have been impelled towards a study of a

9 In order of publication the main works are: P. Van Tieghem, *Introduction à l'étude d'Emile Zola: 'Germinal'* (*Documents inédits de la Bibliothèque nationale*, Paris, C.D.U., 1954); I.-M. Frandon, *Autour de 'Germinal': la mine et les mineurs* (Geneva, Droz, 1955); E. M. Grant, *Zola's 'Germinal': A Critical and Historical Study* (Leicester U.P., 1962); R. H. Zakarian, *Zola's 'Germinal': A Critical Study of its Primary Sources* (Geneva, Droz, 1972).

mining area by a meeting and discussions in the summer of 1883 with
Alfred Giard, a left-wing *député* representing Valenciennes, an industrial
constituency with a strong mining element. When *La Joie de vivre* was
completed towards the end of November 1883, the project for his
second novel on the working class comes to the surface, not without
hesitations and with a colouring very different from the final composition. Edmond de Goncourt's *Journal* has an entry for 16 January 1884:

> Il est embarrassé à propos du roman qu'il doit faire maintenant, *Les
> Paysans*. . . . *Les Chemins de fer*, son roman sur le mouvement d'une
> gare, et la monographie d'un bonhomme vivant dans ce mouvement,
> avec un drame quelconque . . . ce roman, il ne le voit pas dans ce
> moment-ci. . . . Il serait plus porté à faire quelque chose se rapportant
> à une grève dans un pays de mine, et qui débuterait par un bourgeois
> égorgé à la première page . . . puis le jugement . . . des hommes
> condamnés à mort, d'autres à la prison . . . et parmi les débats du
> procès, l'introduction d'une sérieuse et approfondie étude de la question
> sociale.

This entry reveals a good deal of Zola's attitudes on the eve of his
beginning the active foraging for 'documents'. We find three projects
churning round in the novelist's mind, all of which he will ultimately
complete over the next six years: *La Terre*, *La Bête humaine* and *Germinal*.
If *La Terre* had been undertaken at this stage it may well have turned
into a study of politics as it applied to the peasantry during a period of
agricultural crisis—there are hints of this in the electoral scenes in *La
Terre*. Instead, Zola retains the notion of economic crisis and examines
its effects not on the peasantry but on the industrial worker. The project
for the railway novel which is to become *La Bête humaine* is still exceed-
ingly vague in his mind. The more concrete details which Zola attributes
to his mining novel will be transferred virtually *en bloc* to *La Bête
humaine*, notably the 'bourgeois égorgé' and the trial scenes. Hence,
however, the accumulation of a good deal of material in the dossiers of
*Germinal* relating to the trial and condemnation of striking workers
which, ultimately, Zola does not need. Hence, too, the curious over-
lapping at moments of Etienne Lantier with the pathological hero of
*La Bête humaine* which we will discuss in the section on psychology.

Zola's documentary note-taking is squeezed into the short period
from the second half of January until the beginning of the composition
of the novel on 2 April 1884. During the same period he also manages
an outline sketch of the main lines of the novel (*Ebauche*), works out a

first plan, the characters, and a first detailed chapter plan. The creation
of the novel goes on side by side with the documentation.

The work on which Zola drew most, and certainly the one which
appealed most to his imagination, was a factual work of popularization
by Louis-Laurent Simonin—*La Vie souterraine, ou les mines et les mineurs*
(1867), whose text and illustrations acted as a strong stimulus and as
'objective' support for much of the last part of the novel, describing the
disaster and the flooding of the mine. Although the horrifying catastrophe in Part VII presents us with an intensely personal Zolaesque
vision, we can see here how the documentation functions as a controlling
and justifying factor for the novelist, raising personal neurosis to the
status of a general phenomenon and 'allowing' him to use it in the novel.
Other episodes such as the lowering of the horse into the pit, the Tartaret
description and that of the abandoned mine-shaft also have their source
in Simonin.

About a dozen other works are referred to in Zola's notes; each
contributes something, though it is not true to say as does Van Tieghem
that Zola notes only what he will use in the novel. Important scenes
evolve from, or are paralleled by, Zola's notes on E. Dormoy, *Topo-
graphie souterraine du bassin houiller de Valenciennes* (1867), E. de Laveleye,
*Le Socialisme contemporain* (2nd edn, 1883), P. Leroy-Beaulieu, *La
Question ouvrière au XIX$^e$ siècle* (1872), O. Testut, *L'Internationale: son
origine, son but, son caractère . . .* (1871), Y. Guyot, *La Science économique*
(1881). Three novels were published a short while before the composition
of *Germinal* and were situated entirely or in part in mining communities:
H. Malot, *Sans famille* (1878), M. Talmeyr, *Le Grisou* (1880), Y. Guyot,
*Scènes de l'enfer social. La famille Pichot* (1882). Zola was acquainted with
these works, but only the last can be shown to have had clear influence
on the composition of *Germinal*.

The greatest single mass of documents influencing Zola's novel is his
own series of notes taken during his visit to Anzin, a visit which lasted
something between a week and a fortnight beginning on 23 February
1884. This visit was improvised after news had arrived in Paris of a
miners' strike in the north of France which had broken out on 19
February. Zola, passing himself off as a secretary of his friend Alfred
Giard, was able to penetrate the social and political life of the community
at this moment of stress, as well as being able to visit a mine and have
explained to him the technicalities of the industry. The resulting notes
which constitute somewhere between a third and a half of the documentation are stuffed with detail and go to form the authentic

background to the novel, especially that of the establishing scenes in Parts I and II. The *Notes sur Anzin* are more than the raw materials for the novel taking shape in Zola's mind, they are a mixture of artist's impressions, facts, details, gestures, vocabulary, confused and repetitive it is true, but already being worked on imaginatively. They are sketches, in the sense that an artist will sketch aspects of his subject before putting the whole picture on to canvas.

## The Ebauche

The outline sketch for the novel (*Ebauche*)[10] is Zola's first attempt to see the work as a totality. It is not, however, isolated from the 'documentary' preparation of the novel, since part of it was composed before the visit to Anzin and part after. One can thus see the *Notes sur Anzin* as making concrete some of the notions in the early part of the *Ebauche*, and then changing somewhat the direction of the later part. The distinction between 'documentation' and 'creation' is an unreal one, they are both part of the same imaginative but ordering process. Zola starts his sketch by stating the theme of his work:

> Le roman est le soulèvement des salariés, le coup d'épaule donné à la société, qui craque un instant: en un mot la lutte du capital et du travail. C'est là qu'est l'importance du livre, je le veux prédisant l'avenir, posant la question la plus importante du vingtième siècle.

We shall see later that Zola transforms this socio-political intention into a drama at once more personal and more cosmic. For the moment, however, the mention of the twentieth century is sufficient indication that Zola is more concerned with addressing a message to the society of the mid 1880s than with a narrowly-defined historicity which would relate it simply to the mid 1860s which is the date when the novel is supposed to be taking place. His aim is no longer, as it was at the beginning of his series, to provide a picture and analysis of the Second Empire, but rather to use that period as a convenient framework for a critique of contemporary society, even though the Empire had fallen and been replaced by the Third Republic. This intention in the *Ebauche* is maintained in the novel and comes to the surface during the strikers' hunger riots in the famous 'vision rouge de la révolution qui les emporterait tous, fatalement, par une soirée sanglante de cette fin de siècle' (334).

[10] Published in full in E. M. Grant, *op. cit.*, 171–206, from which the unattributed quotations in this section are taken.

It is only at a second stage that characters begin slowly to invade this outline scenario: 'Voilà la carcasse en grand. Seulement, il faut mettre là-dedans des personnages et les faire agir.' Zola's language here is significant of the extent to which he thinks of his novel as a study of a social problem, the characters being as it were dropped into the problem and churned about mainly in order to define better the contours of the problem. Such an attitude lends support to the idea that at this point in the creative process Zola is more interested in general phenomena than in individual psychology.

In analysing the capital versus labour theme, Zola concentrates initially on the capitalist aspect, debating whether to have it incarnated in a small mine-owner or in a large-scale company represented locally by a manager, and decides in the end to have both. The small-scale enterprise is to be included to show 'les pertes communes, souffrance des ouvriers et ruine du capital . . .', the large company in order to be 'plus actuel, plus large . . .'. It is perhaps surprising that only one page out of the first eleven of Zola's manuscript *Ebauche* is concerned with describing the problem from the workers' viewpoint, and then only in the most general terms. Politics are not mentioned, the variety of working-class Movements being sketched in only after the visit to Anzin. At first, all the weight is given to abstract terms of struggle, defeat and revenge. The conclusion of the novel is, initially, pessimistic, closer to the vision which will ultimately be attributed to Souvarine:

La secousse donnée à la société qui a craqué, et faire prévoir d'autres secousses jusqu'à l'effondrement final.

No hint is given of the germination image which emerges so strongly in the last page of the finished novel.

The *Ebauche* is perceived by Zola as a series of logical deductions from the theme given in the first paragraph quoted above. It is liberally sprinkled with words which underline the fact: 'Donc . . . alors . . . par conséquent . . . conclusion logique . . .', etc. This, in spite of repetitions, re-workings, and hesitations. Such insistence on logic is the carrying over into the preparation of the novel of the precepts of the naturalist novelist as scientific inquirer, and emerges in the end in the solid, constructed feeling of the work.

The relative abstractness of the opening pages of the *Ebauche* does not prevent Zola from including already some of the images which will illuminate the novel. The picture of society splitting under stress is included in the first sentence and repeated later. This is the starting-point for its diversification in the novel into pictures of splitting, cracking, falling apart and collapse, which reaches its height as the result of the engulfing of the Voreux pit (VII, 3).

Another image, this time relatively elaborate, which occurs to Zola very early on is the expression used to describe the major shareholders and board of directors of the company in Paris:

> . . . je laisserai de côté les actionnaires, les comités, etc., pour en faire une sorte de tabernacle reculé, de dieu vivant et mangeant les ouvriers dans l'ombre.

He wants the Company's statements to be

> 'comme un oracle qui parle, une force inconnue et terrible . . .',

retouches the image later, turning the 'société anonyme' (so much more ambiguous than the English 'limited company'!) into a 'dieu muet et impitoyable', before its final form as 'dieu capital, accroupi dans son temple, comme une bête grasse et repue, monstrueuse d'assouvissement'. But neither the image of splitting apart, nor that of Capital, seen as a beast inspiring religious terror, is created specially for use in *Germinal*, and both can be found elsewhere in Zola's works. The 'tabernacle' image, for example, is already present in *La Curée*, written thirteen years earlier, where it is used to describe the head offices of the Crédit viticole:

> . . . le temple grave et digne de l'argent; et rien ne frappait le public d'une émotion plus religieuse, que le sanctuaire, que la Caisse, où conduisait un corridor d'une nudité sacrée, et où l'on apercevait le coffre-fort, le dieu accroupi, scellé au mur, trapu et dormant, avec ses trois serrures, ses flancs épais, son air de brute divine.[11]

Capital is a monster of Zola's imagination. Its attributes—devouring, digesting or sleeping, squatting—suggest a creature of nightmare defined largely by its mouth, belly and gut. At the same time, however, it is immobilized in a religious-type sanctuary. One has only to compare this picture with Balzac's evocation of the characteristics of the 'toute-puissante pièce de cent sous' in *La Cousine Bette*[12] which is characterized by its life, its beauty, its energy, its mobility, to see that underneath the personal obsession of Zola there is also a description of a different stage of capitalism from that of Balzac. Money in Balzac's novels is surging upwards and out into the world, conquering new domains; in Zola's

---

[11] Zola, *Les Rougon-Macquart* (Pléiade), vol. I, 417–18.
[12] Balzac, *La Comédie humaine* (Pléiade), vol. VI, 400.

images quoted above it has already conquered all and now needs only steady feeding. This image does not eliminate others describing individual capitalists' activities (in *La Curée*, for example) as feverish and fevered, but they are merely the infected servants of this god of Capital.

Another important feature of the *Ebauche*, which again places emphasis on a continuity of inspiration in Zola's works, is the insistence on the need for a drama of strong contrasts and violence, intended to induce a shudder in the bourgeois reader. We have already seen how, in the preparatory notes for the Rougon-Macquart series, Zola required such drama. This same desire is evident not only in the stage vocabulary in the *Ebauche*:

> . . . un drame peut-être, une fille séduite, etc., de façon à dramatiser ce côté de l'action et obtenir un dénouement à la fin. . . .

but also in the conception of individual scenes, such as in the staccato notation of the reactions of the bourgeois household isolated by the strikers: 'Peur, drame, maison attaquée, dangers courus, défense, mort peut-être.' This general need for strong drama in Zola is reinforced in the case of *Germinal* by the fact that the idea of writing a play on the subject appears to have occurred to him *before* that of writing a novel. Therefore, as Martin Kanes has written[13] 'the play represents a step in the creation of *Germinal*'. If some parts of *Germinal* seem melodramatic, it is not simply because Zola likes melodrama but also because the first notion, of which the *Ebauche* retains strong traces, was for the composition of a melodrama, literally speaking:

> . . . in its first and most elementary form, *Germinal* appears as a typical boulevard melodrama, complete with an admirable hero, a pathetic heroine, a traitor, a villain . . . a conflict of sensational violence in a striking décor. . . .[14]

In the end a play was indeed composed, but only after the publication of the novel.

It is natural that there should be a good number of hesitations in the *Ebauche*. We find, for example, hesitations over the role and importance of Etienne, hesitations over the placing of the catastrophic collapse of the pit, and a good many others. The hesitations are not, however,

[13] '*Germinal*: drama and dramatic structure', *Modern Philology* LXI (1) (August 1963), 12–25.

[14] *Ibid.*, 16.

those of timidity, but of shaping. Zola follows up an idea for a scene, then stands back to see how it will go into the overall pattern. If unsatisfied he simply ploughs on, setting aside a scene which may be strong with the words 'Je reprends', 'On recommence', 'Cela est à voir'. The one major element missing from the *Ebauche* is the personality of the mine. It is difficult to explain why this should be so when its brooding and monstrous presence dominates so much of the atmosphere of the finished work. One can only tentatively propose that even for such a methodical novelist as Zola, a good deal nevertheless depends on the act of writing. All the background and preparation in the world does not, cannot, fully explain the novel.

# 2. The Novel

Before touching on questions of social description and conflict, ideologies and themes, *Germinal* hits us as an atmosphere: blackness, bleakness, earth more liquid than solid, a sort of cosmic broth gone dead; the only defining element the straight-line road drawing along it a man. The man's first observations to emerge from this shadowy world are a sense of numbness, then of fear. The three fires which appear, disappear, reappear, the gigantic and fantastic set of buildings—not yet perceived as a mine—animated by breathings from an invisible source, have much in common with the blasted heath of *Macbeth* as a place of doubt and uncertainty, fear, monstrosity and blackness.

But to see the opening paragraphs of the novel only in these terms is to distort their sense. The atmosphere described above is that felt by Etienne, an Etienne representing that part of Zola which was subject to such anxieties. There is another part of the sense represented by those observations which calm the anxieties by relating them to specific causes: the blackness and bleakness—3 a.m. on a windy night in March between Marchiennes and Montsou; the numbness—the man is inadequately clad for the season; the force of the abstract 'tout disparut' is reduced to human proportions by the subsequent explanation—the man is now walking between a fence on one side and a grassy bank on the other; and so on. The passage is in fact bifocal, at once rational and irrational. There is, however, no systematic separation of points of view such as one finds in, say, Flaubert's *Education sentimentale* where the description of the 1848 Revolution is not an attempt at a rational or objective explanation of the events by the narrator combined with the subjective explanation by the hero, but simply a partial view of the events seen through the eyes of Frédéric Moreau, the hero, who becomes the sole, but biased, guarantor of what is observed. In Zola's novel one cannot make a simple equation of Etienne with the irrational point of view and of the narrator with the rational one. Zola has blurred the edges of the point of view technique in order to have Etienne explain the details of the mine and, later, of the mining community, while at the same time using him to express the primitive fears of man in the face of 'l'inconnu' or 'les ténèbres'. Much of the strength of the novel comes from the coincidence of the social theme with a setting which also permits full exploration of the irrational. Etienne is the character in whom these two aspects converge and it seems appropriate therefore to begin the study of the novel proper with him.

*A study in psychology: Etienne*

The earliest version[1] of the genealogical tree of the Rougon-Macquart family established in 1869 includes Etienne Lantier, though the characteristics ascribed to him may surprise the reader of *Germinal*: 'Meurtrier. Hérédité de l'ivrognerie se tournant en folie.' At this date, Etienne is intended for 'un roman qui aura pour cadre le monde judiciaire . . . un roman de cour d'assises . . .'. This picture is maintained in two subsequent versions of the family tree: the second version of 1869 gives: 'Influence de l'ivrognerie des parents poussant un enfant au meurtre'; then, the 1878 version of *Une Page d'amour* reads: 'Hérédité de l'ivrognerie se tournant en folie homicide. Etat de crime.' In addition, the young Etienne, illegitimate son of Gervaise Macquart and Lantier, has been mentioned in passing in *L'Assommoir*, working in Lille with the railways. This, then, is the general outline picked up by Zola in 1884 when he begins serious work on *Germinal*.

The first mention of Etienne in the *Ebauche* of *Germinal* describes him as the lover of Catherine. As for his profession, Zola would prefer to keep him as an engine-man but sees he will have to fix things so as

[1] Bibliothèque nationale MS.; n.a.f. 10345, f. 130.

to have him work underground. The one constant feature, however, is that Etienne is a 'maniaque de l'assassinat' and will probably carry out one or even two murders, one at least being the murder of a daughter of a mine-owner or manager.

It is only after the visit to Anzin that other aspects of Etienne begin to come to the forefront. His role in the novel becomes more important. His love for Catherine is discussed again. In addition, his work underground and his experience of the general industrial crisis is now to shape 'son éducation de socialiste'. This phrase is then repeated several times in the *Ebauche*. He also acquires the important technical role in the novel of observer and guarantor of the reality of the descriptions: 'Etienne devient mon lien conducteur pour exposer toute la mine . . .'. But the basic character remains unchanged:

> Je veux en faire un révolté, un criminel plus tard. . . . Enfin, il faut le faire sortir de la mine, encore plus révolté qu'il n'y entre, le préparer pour le crime de mon roman sur les chemins de fer, et surtout pour la Commune.

These varied and to some extent conflicting elements are summed up in the expression: 'Homme très complexe dans une nature simple.'

It is only at the very end of the *Ebauche* and also as a sort of *postscriptum* to the character-sketch of Etienne, that Etienne becomes truly central to the novel, and his homicidal tendencies are reduced, though never eliminated. Greater emphasis is now placed on his political education and on the study of the psychology of a labour leader:

> Ses études, sa demi-science, son affinement; ses luttes terribles contre ce qu'il sent qu'il faudrait savoir; son ambition et son naïf orgueil aussi. . . .

He has evolved into

> Tout un personnage central maintenant, beaucoup plus mouvementé. Un héros enfin.

Thus, the evolution of the character of Etienne in the preparatory stages of the novel is, broadly speaking, from the physiological (heredity of alcoholism and violence leading to murder) to the sociological (the man defined by his work situation and self-education). The original characterization persists mainly in vestigial form in the novel—it is suggested early on (46–7) as an echo of the world of *L'Assommoir*, and recurs in Etienne's gin drinking during the rioting. One scene only reflects the original Etienne—the murder of Chaval. This murder is included by Zola under compulsions which we will discuss later.

When Zola comes to the composition of the sketch for *La Bête humaine* five years later, a study among other things of a compulsive murderer in a novel on railway life, he picks up the threads of the original characterization of Etienne: 'Je n'ai absolument, comme héros à employer, qu'Etienne Lantier, mon Etienne de *Germinal*.' Zola was in fact stuck with his predetermined family tree and initially tried to make the best of a nearly incompatible set of characteristics in his new novel, persisting in using Etienne virtually throughout the preparatory stages of *La Bête humaine*. However, in spite of the murder of Chaval, Etienne is not a homicidal maniac, and is not reduced to an uncontrollable blood lust every time he is sexually excited. Zola creates, therefore, for this seventeenth novel of his series, and almost *in extremis*, a new brother, Jacques Lantier, and transfers to him in their entirety the characteristics originally attributed to Etienne. This illustrates well the interesting gap in Zola's works between his original intentions and actual execution, a gap which is produced in the case of *Germinal* not simply by the creative instincts of the novelist in the heat of composition but also by the direct experience of the strike at Anzin and conversations with the miners' leader Emile Basly and others in the mining area.

A further element, not specifically alluded to in the *Ebauche* or in the character-sketch of the hero, which forms part of the make-up of Etienne can be deduced from his ultimate fate mentioned in *Le Docteur Pascal*. Having realized how incompatible the Etienne of *Germinal* had become with the themes of *La Bête humaine* and having thus eliminated him from the latter work, Zola does not simply leave him as we see him at the end of *Germinal*, marching off into a nebulous future as a full-time trade union organizer, perhaps along the lines of a Pluchart, an exhausted organizer of meetings, a travelling-salesman of the Revolution. He is described as returning to Paris and being

> compromis plus tard dans l'insurrection de la Commune, dont il avait défendu les idées avec emportement; on l'avait condamné à mort, puis gracié et déporté, de sorte qu'il se trouvait maintenant à Nouméa. . . .

In this South Pacific exile he marries and has a daughter. This involvement in the Commune is the last trace of Zola's original intention of keeping Etienne for his novel on the Commune. The language used, however, is subdued and does not suggest any wildly criminal excess on

Etienne's part. One senses that Etienne is still essentially the dreamer caught up in politics and then driven out of his depth. The nearest parallel to such a personality in Zola's works is the character of Florent in *Le Ventre de Paris*, the third novel of the Rougon-Macquart series. Florent is caught up in the street fighting at the time of Napoleon III's *coup d'état*, is captured and deported, returning some years later to devote himself to a conspiracy which is totally ineffectual and is deported once again. This early picture of the dreamer-cum-revolutionary provides a stereotype to which Etienne in many ways conforms, down to their common use of language like 'les maigres mangeant les gras' (428) to express a Darwinian-type struggle for existence, and including even attitudes to sexual drives and their relation to politics. For both Florent and Etienne have a side to their character which makes them virtual monks of the revolution, chaste to the point of prudishness, with the suggestion that revolutionary energy is pent up or diverted sexual energy.

These two notions, then, the ineffectual dreamer-revolutionary (Florent) and the violent criminal (Jacques Lantier) exist as the buried possibilities available for the portrait of Etienne. Both outcrop in him from time to time.

But it is as an eye and a registering instrument that Etienne first strikes the reader, an observer of the outside world and a reactor to it. Furthermore, his reactions project an emotional colouring on to the outside world which in its turn provokes new reactions so that there is a circular linking of cause and effect which draws the initially external observer into a much closer and living relationship with the world observed. Etienne's first observations give us an 'apparition fantastique' (8) which is then emotionally devalued, rendered harmless, by being designated as 'une fosse' (8). An exchange of factual information, then a description, do not entirely quieten the emotional sensitivities of Etienne who, in spite of the purely physical preoccupations attributed to him on the first page of the novel ('Une seule idée occupait sa tête vide . . . l'espoir que le froid serait moins vif . . .') is revealed as an 'homme qui se sentait regardé', and seeks reassurance from another human being that the rationalization of his fears is in fact well-founded ('C'est une fosse, n'est-ce pas?') (9). Only when he gains this approval does the pit begin in his mind to belong to the material world: 'Le Voreux, à présent, sortait du rêve.' Even then, however, the straightforward description of the mine buildings soon lurches back into the world of myth with the sentence

Cette fosse, tassée au fond d'un creux . . . sa cheminée comme une corne menaçante . . . un air mauvais de bête goulue, accroupie là pour manger le monde. (9)

This in turn provokes another attempt at gaining reassurance by the repetition of the magic phrase 'Oui, c'était bien une fosse . . .' (10) and the finding of an explanation for the regular breathing of the monster. The culmination of this opening scene, which provides us with an insight into the nature of the vision of Zola himself, shows us Etienne isolated on the top of the spoil heap sensing intuitively the prevailing spirit of the area:

Et, les yeux errants, il s'efforçait de percer les ombres, tourmenté du désir et de la peur de voir. (11)

Desire to see and fear of seeing are the roots of Etienne's vision, both of the world around him and the world inside himself.

Once Zola has established this perspective, it then gives way to the Etienne as neutral observer, the functional role of 'lien conducteur' mentioned in the *Ebauche*. He acts as an interviewer of Bonnemort, nudging him gently into giving his family history and, incidentally, that of the mine. This curious dropping of the emotional charge from Etienne's characterization and the transference to Bonnemort of some of the figures of speech by which it was translated ('le sang bu et les os avalés par les roches'—14) reveals a similarity in the portrayal of nominally separate individual characters in the name of the superior importance of the total vision of the mine, which invades in similar fashion the consciousness of all the miners. This is close to saying that Zola's portrait of the psychology of individuals is either defective or subordinate to the influence of environment, and throws up the whole question of Zola as a psychological novelist, to which we shall return at the end of this section.

Etienne is next seen exploring the pithead buildings and experiencing the journey to work underground (I, 3). He wanders around the buildings which turn into an animate labyrinth,[2] full of 'trous noirs, inquiétants avec la complication de leurs salles et de leurs étages' (26). Eyes watch him, machines attract him 'dans le remuement de toutes ces choses noires et bruyantes qui s'agitaient' (27). Gradually Etienne becomes accustomed to the darkness and the shapes in the unnatural lighting, and registers them with his eyes and ears in disjointed fashion. This helps

[2] For a fascinating study of this aspect of Zola's work, see M. Maurin, 'Zola's labyrinths', *Yale French Studies* 42 (June 1969), 89–104.

him to regain some contact with the everyday world, but not to any great extent. The sense he does make of his surroundings is by peopling the darkness with frightening apparitions, the cable running out and being compared to the soundless rushing flight of a bird, the cage pouncing silently out of the pit like some nocturnal animal of prey, and the dominant image once again of the mine swallowing the miners, devouring its ration of human flesh. This process is repeated in the second half of the chapter with the actual descent into the mine. All normal sense data are upset:

> tout sombra . . . vertige anxieux . . . n'ayant plus la perception nette de ses sensations . . . la peur d'une catastrophe . . . les lampes éclairaient mal. . . . (34)

A precarious foothold on everyday reality is kept by this flickering and inadequate light and by the voices and bits of information given to him by the other miners. Once at pit bottom we have the recurrence of detailed notation mixed with ominous life around, the former barely keeping at bay the latter. This attitude which sees spirits, and in this case largely evil spirits, in inanimate and man-made objects transfers to late nineteenth-century industrial man the modes of thought normally associated with primitive religions. They mediate and reduce our fears of our surroundings. Zola, implicitly here and much more explicitly in *La Bête humaine* where it is the dominant characteristic of Jacques Lantier, shows this trait continuing to exist as a permanent element in the human psyche. To this extent Etienne is simply another representative of 'physiological' man as Zola saw him, a complex of basic appetites and instincts undermined by neurotic fears and anxieties.

When one turns away from the aspect of Etienne defined by the nature of his perception of reality and begins to look at his physical presence and conscious thought processes, one finds more of the traditional aspects of characterization in him. He is small and dark, both his parents coming from Provence, and contrasts strongly with the blonde-haired, slow-tempered people of the Nord.[3] He is portrayed as a rather hasty individual, having been sacked for striking his previous foreman. His coming from outside the community of Montsou provides a motive for his clearer observation of the true state of the miners' existence,

[3] Le Nord is of course the name of the *département* in which the action takes place, and does not designate the north of France in general. Chaval, for example, comes from the *département* of the Pas-de-Calais, also in the north of France, but is a different 'racial' type again.

provokes the reaction that something must be done about the situation, and begins the process of political education which culminates in his leadership of the strike.

Etienne's sense of revolt at the condition of the miners is revealed initially not by a process of psychological analysis but by his physical reactions to the situation as he observes it and as it is being described to him. He is shown as 'frémissant', not as the agent of his reactions, but as their vehicle: 'une révolte lente le soulevait' (54–5). This is again a consequence of naturalist theory, which eliminates the initiating value of thought. Etienne is shown as reacting, the reader is free if he wishes to infer some sort of psychological activity accompanying the actions, but cannot give it precedence over this revolt of the whole organic being. Ultimately, this picture of Etienne is in harmony with the notion of revolution 'germinating', growing as naturally in a mining community enduring such exploitation as a seed grows in the earth.

The 'natural' reaction crystallizes round the specific issue of the disguised reduction in wages and, for Etienne, leads to the decision to organize a strike, which is coupled with the realization that he must also educate himself. The education takes two forms, one the acquisition of a theoretical background for his arguments, the other the acquisition of the practical tactics of a labour organizer. It is hardly necessary to stress how disorganized Etienne's education is; we should rather point out the difficulty of its being anything but disorganized at such a period in time, and in a community so spiritually isolated as that of Montsou. At a time when social histories, let alone social histories of the working class, were hardly being written, even less assimilated by the working class, it was inevitable that there should be a strong dose of the arbitrary and unverified in virtually any attempt at self-education. And this is the case with Etienne. Some of the theoretical education and most of the tactics are suggested by his correspondence with Pluchart, who is his sole educated contact outside Montsou. The rest is made up by his day-to-day working experience and by his discussions with Rasseneur and Souvarine in the café, which, if it does not have the formality of the venues of the societies for mutual improvement so common in Victorian England, has the same atmosphere of earnestness and performs the same function.

One result of the education Etienne acquires is a sense of difference from the miners around him. He begins to acquire certain refinements and a bourgeois sense of culture which separates him from his comrades. This process of uprooting and separation from an original class as a result of education recurs as a theme much exploited by British writers in the 1950s,[4] though in their case largely as the result of the impact of first-generation university education. Etienne's education from books is telescoped into a relatively short period of time and is little more than sketched in by Zola. What is moving is the picture of the inadequately prepared working-class intellectual, trying out his theories in the various stages of the strike and being carried away by his position as popular tribune into betraying the tentativeness of his own attitudes. Zola shows how the original noble impulse of the 'orgueil d'homme', the notion that 'I, too, am a man and have rights' is partly transformed into an egotistical form of pride.

Etienne's notions of the purpose of social revolution remain constant, if vague. They are essentially dreams, utopian dreams of justice, and in this he resembles one of the 'buried models', the Florent of *Le Ventre de Paris*. He is able to communicate these dreams to the other miners, even though both he and they are aware of the unreality of the dreams. They are a sort of refuge, a paradise of the mind in which one can seek peace and relaxation from the tensions caused by work and grinding poverty, as for example they affect la Maheude:

> Elle finissait par sourire, l'imagination éveillée, entrant dans ce monde merveilleux de l'espoir. Il était si doux d'oublier pendant une heure la réalité triste! . . . il faut bien un coin de mensonge . . . l'idée de la justice. (162)

Etienne, however, never resolves the eternal political problem of the means to be employed to attain these utopian ends.

The confidence in his newly-acquired philosophy, combined with his newly-attained standing in the community, results in Etienne becoming not only a dreamer of dreams for the community, but also for himself. The dream of universal justice is at moments diminished to becoming the dream of a career, with Etienne as the first working man to be elected to the Chambre des Députés. Zola shows Etienne oscillating between the poles of visionary and careerist, though very little in the way of transition is attempted to explain the oscillation. The result is saved from becoming an ill-assorted assemblage of stock characteristics by the presence in the character of a basic insecurity which, paradoxically, acts as a unifying element. We have seen how, in observing the outside

[4] Richard Hoggart, Raymond Williams, John Wain, Kingsley Amis, have all in their different ways testified to the culture-shock produced by increased education, and described its product, the rootless intellectual.

world, Etienne moves from peopling it with monsters to using description or naming of objects in order to control his sense of anxiety which nevertheless persists in invading his picture of it. Similarly, in the political world the movement from utopianism to careerism, dream to reality, is a constantly renewed casting round for a fixed point to which he can attach himself, for fear of being invaded by a sense of his own inadequacy:

> Aussi, à certaines heures de bon sens, éprouvait-il une inquiétude sur sa mission, la peur de n'être point l'homme attendu. (217)

Etienne drives himself on, it seems, for fear of looking into his fears.

This fluctuating, almost neurotic, behaviour is at its clearest in his sexual life. The sexual sub-plot revolving round Etienne, Chaval and Catherine was the starting-point for Etienne's inclusion in the novel. At one level it has all the characteristics of melodrama with its violence and sentimentality, with Etienne as a pure and noble hero, Chaval the brutal villain, and Catherine, with more than a touch of Little Nell about her, the pitiful victim in need of salvation. Already in the *Ebauche*, however, Etienne is seen as having two major aspects to his character, his love for Catherine and his political education, with both being undermined by 'un inconnu terrible chez lui', his inherited neurosis forcing him to kill. Zola intended eradicating sentimentality from Etienne's love, and does it by reference to the love of Goujet for Gervaise in *L'Assommoir*:

> . . . je ne voudrais pas d'un amour à la Goujet, platonique et pleurard. Il veut Catherine, et s'il ne la prend pas, c'est qu'il y a des obstacles.

Something of this brutal aspect persists in Etienne's *intentions*, but from the earliest scenes in the novel he is already described as 'intimidé', in spite of being tormented by desire (the melodramatic language is appropriate here). The torment is increased by Chaval's intervention during Etienne's first day down the mine, brutally kissing Catherine in front of Etienne, and further inhibiting him. The contrast between the virile, whiskered and diabolical Chaval and an Etienne at this stage weak, nervous and unsure of himself is stressed. A good deal of the plot is then devoted to trying to reverse this situation, which recurs obsessively in Zola's works, namely winning the love of a woman who has loved, or at least been taken, by another man first. This type of situation[5] has its clearest expression in Zola's early novel *Madeleine Férat* written well

[5] For an excellent analysis of the Œdipal aspect of *Madeleine Férat*, see J. Borie, *Zola et les mythes . . .* (Seuil, 1971), 53–63.

before the start of the Rougon-Macquart series. The drama of frustration as it comes to be revealed in *Germinal* is far more complex than the initial idea of an eternal triangle dealing with love and jealousy in violent terms.

Certain scenes in the novel are privileged as far as the study of the sexual psychology of Etienne is concerned. They are not the moments when Zola interpolates a few lines of 'analysis' to show the stage reached in the relations between Etienne, Chaval and Catherine, but moments when Zola projects in visual terms an equivalent of the anguish of Etienne. Two examples: first, the scene (II, 5) in which Etienne after his first day down the mine and the establishment of the rivalry between him and Chaval, walks round the abandoned pit, Réquillart. The psychological strain in Etienne is suggested initially in physiological terms: 'il éprouvait un tel malaise, une telle pesanteur de tête . . .' (116). He is feverish, and one accepts at first the straightforward reason—an excessive fatigue causing a bout of fever. This detail Zola had extracted from one of his documentary sources on illnesses in the mining industry. As the chapter progresses, however, Etienne becomes quite clearly more and more afflicted by the general promiscuity he observes in the grounds of the old workings. His tense reactions come as a contrast to the relaxed, 'natural' and erotically unaware reactions on the part of le vieux Mouque, who is seen here in comic terms as preoccupied merely with not tripping over the couples and whose only worry is that one couple is beginning to weaken his bedroom wall by their activities. When Etienne observes Philomène and Zacharie, then the trio Jeanlin-Lydie-Bébert—an infantile and degenerate prefiguration of his own situation—his meditations are initially rational, partly reflecting the bourgeois ideology of the time, and bear on the social implications of promiscuity:

> Que de misère! et toutes ces filles, éreintées de fatigue, qui étaient encore assez bêtes, le soir, pour fabriquer des petits, de la chair à travail et à souffrance! (123)

This, however, is only the prelude to a more intimate, personal reflection which Zola suggests but steadfastly refuses to analyse. What he does is to find an atmospheric equivalent to Etienne's mental state:

> Le temps mou l'étouffait un peu, des gouttes de pluie, rares encore, tombaient sur ses mains fiévreuses. (123)

When Chaval and Catherine arrive unrecognized by Etienne, he is 'envahi d'un malaise, d'une sorte d'excitation jalouse où montait de la

colère' (126). When he does recognize who it is, his role changes from
that of observer, albeit feverish, to that of *voyeur*. He hides in the
shadows, he spies, and has a guilty sense of infringing taboos. He feels
it is weakness on his part and reacts in a fury of frustration at what he is
witnessing. Again, the desire to see and fear of seeing results in a personal
vision which Etienne can barely control.

A similar scene of frustrated and exasperated sexuality concerns
Etienne and Catherine (III, 3), and suggests one temporary solution to
the problem, at least as far as Etienne is concerned. Etienne, installed
in the Maheu household, sleeps in the same room as Catherine and is
embarrassed by the situation. We are now equally far away both from
the Etienne of the *Ebauche*, brutal and only prevented by obstacles from
taking Catherine, and from the Etienne *à la* Goujet with his sentimental
and platonic love. What we have is a strongly sexed Etienne prevented
from taking Catherine by obstacles within his own mind. Once again
the eye of Etienne shifts from merely observing or reflecting the world
to being an organ of the *voyeur* mingling visual and mental images, and
is used to stand for both objective and subjective modes of perception:

> ... une sorte d'obsession le faisait, malgré lui, guetter de l'œil l'instant
> où elle se couchait ... (155)

This obsession is fixed on erotically charged actions of Catherine un-
dressing and pinning up her hair and glimpses of her body, her white
flesh, a knee, her breasts. Once again the mechanism of partial release
from the obsession-repression cycle is in voyeurism which leaves an
exasperated residue of feeling. The presence of Catherine's parents is
another factor which cripples the 'natural' emotional response, and
produces guilt feelings. Release is obtained temporarily from the
distressing awareness of sexuality by retreating into the childhood
world of *camaraderie*:

> ils préféraient les soirs de tranquillité, où ils se mettaient à l'aise, en
> camarades. (156)

This demonstration of the psychological strains undergone by Etienne
modulates in the same chapter from the 'private' to the 'public' key:
'Ce fut l'époque où Etienne entendit les idées qui bourdonnaient dans
son crâne' (157). The political activities of Etienne provide to some
extent relief from his personal tensions, and at the same time act as a
parallel to them. He experiences an instinctive sense of revolt, and
although his self-education begins to give him a renewed sense of

confidence, his worries about the gaps in his knowledge and the in-adequacy of his understanding cause him to adopt a regressive attitude, to ignore his difficulties and retreat into a child-like dream world of 'la régénération radicale des peuples, sans que cela dût coûter une vitre cassée ni une goutte de sang' (158).

It would certainly be forcing the interpretation to say that Etienne sublimates personal activities in political activity, for the importance of other influences is certainly paramount. Nevertheless there is in his politics an element of sexual rivalry with Chaval which is stressed by Zola throughout the novel, leading to the fight between Chaval and Etienne at Rasseneur's (VI, 3) which has as its nominal cause provocative remarks over the strike but which rapidly becomes a struggle between two males for dominance and possession of the female. The fight is conducted in the presence of Catherine, and she is thrown at Etienne at the end as his prize for winning. From this viewpoint the strike is a virility drama.

The *dénouement* of this drama is prevented even after the fight by Catherine's fatalism—'Chaval est mon homme, je n'ai pas à coucher ailleurs que chez lui' (391)—and by a return of a sense of shame between them. It is only reached when the three protagonists are finally totally isolated and trapped in the mine together: 'C'était l'ancienne bataille qui recommençait' (477). The ambiguity of *ancienne* is deliberate, referring to the specific previous quarrel between Etienne and Chaval and at the same time to the archetypal quarrel as of cavemen over possession of the female. Just as the strike has been concluded by a blood-letting, so the private drama must finish in the same way. In killing Chaval, Etienne finally releases the 'poison' of his inheritance, which is not simply that of alcoholism, but above all the primitive urge to kill. His superiority, his virility, is finally established, then consum-mated by making love to Catherine. The last doubts at his own virility are removed for Etienne by the thought that he is the first to make love to Catherine since she has reached puberty. Her association with Chaval was when she was still a child physically, and, therefore, does not count. This sex act, unlikely as it may be given the circumstances, is the necessary act which releases Etienne from his anxieties, his sense of inadequacy, his private monsters, just as he is soon released physically from his trapped position, released too from the infernal world of Montsou. He has not forgotten the 'tristesse immense, la misère des générations, l'excès de douleur où peut tomber la vie', but he is no longer in bondage to it. All this prepares the way for the blossoming of images of springtime, salvation and growth in the last pages of the novel, where once again the social theme rejoins the theme of the individual.

It is hardly necessary to underline the similarities between Zola and his hero, and show how the latter provides the novelist with a dramatic projection of his neuroses, a therapy even. In this it has a great deal in common with its immediate predecessor in the Rougon-Macquart series, *La Joie de vivre*, with its blank terror of death scarcely and only intermittently kept at bay by the affirmation of the powers of life, in spite of permanent suffering. Such an analysis of Etienne cannot, however, be taken as a psychoanalysis of Zola himself, ignoring as it does the political dimension in *Germinal*, which is totally absent from *La Joie de vivre*.

It is a commonplace in the criticism of Zola from his own time to the present day to say that he is no psychologist. Gustave Lanson wrote at the end of the last century in his *Histoire de la littérature française*: 'La psychologie des romans de M. Zola est bien courte.' Martin Turnell, much more recently, has stated that:

> It is common ground among his admirers and critics that Zola was singularly deficient in psychological insight. . . . Zola's characters are, with few exceptions, artificial constructions which betray a remarkable poverty of experience.[6]

What these opinions have in common are certain views of psychology in literature. It is seen either in terms of the classical 'roman d'analyse' which is felt by such critics to deal with descriptions of infinitely subtle and detailed inquiries into states of mind and clashes of mind on mind to the exclusion of virtually everything else—novels such as *La Princesse de Clèves* or Constant's *Adolphe*[7] are typically quoted in such a context — or alternatively in terms of the more earthy 'roman de mœurs', where authors such as Dickens or Balzac are cited as examples of writers who, while lacking the 'refinements' of the classical psychological novelist, are nevertheless capable of creating well-rounded characters, often eccentric, exaggerated or grotesque, but unforgettable. We have thus in the minds of such critics the implicit assumption that only the barely incarnated 'mind' or the rich 'character' can be the model of good

[6] M. Turnell, *The Art of French Fiction* (Hamish Hamilton, 1959), 122–3.

[7] It is clear that neither of these works is only 'psychological' in the sense used here.

psychology in a novel, and that the latter is already more vulgar, less subtle, than the former.

Etienne clearly does not conform to either of these stereotypes. On the other hand, the details we are given of the workings of his mind reveal him as certainly more complex than, say, the character outlines, or 'shadowgraphs' as they have been called, found in the Voltairian *conte*. But to say this is to accept the criteria imposed by the critics quoted above. What Zola has done in the case of Etienne is to privilege other aspects of what can still be called psychology and character. The text of the novel gives by Zola's emphasis on the eye ample material for elaborating notions on Etienne's psychology of perception. The reveries or the hallucinations of Etienne are the end-product of a mingling of external reality with pre-existing mental images. Zola describes the external reality and the dreams or hallucinations, the mental images can thus be deduced. If a great deal of Etienne's conduct is ascribed to basic appetites and instincts, such as aggressiveness or sexuality or both in combination, it is only critics who exist in a pre-Freudian world who can exclude such phenomena from the proper study of psychology. Furthermore, if such instincts are in some degree common to all of us, then Zola can justifiably include them in some form or other in his conception of virtually all his characters, and stress this fact. He certainly loses thereby the qualities of extreme individuality in his characters, but this does not prevent them from having an individuality and a particular psychological configuration. The political education of Etienne is not conducted solely in terms of a clash of ideologies, but is shown to have obscure but definite links with instinctual behaviour. The portrait of Etienne provides also an analysis of the motivation of a political leader, revealing it as a complex of self-seeking and idealistic impulses. All this adds up to the need for a revaluation of Zola as psychologist, and provides some justification, it is hoped, for this long and at first sight slightly perverse insistence on the analysis of the character of Etienne.

## On and about working-class ideologies

In discussing at some length the character of Etienne we have left aside the content of his political education, its relationship to other ideologies expressed in the novel and the implications of Zola's treatment of them. In writing *Germinal* Zola knew he was writing a political novel, and one that was potentially scandalous, one indeed where the scandal was sought. He writes in the *Ebauche*: 'Il faut que le lecteur bourgeois ait un frisson de terreur.' In spite of the political shock of the work, every effort is to be made at presenting, if not an impassive study, at least one going some way towards giving an illusion of impartiality:

> ... des faits, sans plaidoyer ... ne pas tomber dans la revendication bête ... ne sentant pas la haine démocratique. (*Ebauche*)

Once again, one notes the presence in Zola's preparatory work of a strong attempt to apply his scientific naturalist theories to the novel in progress.

The major figures used to study the various aspects of political thought in the working class are Rasseneur, Etienne and Souvarine. The Maheus are used as a litmus test of their success in influencing the working class. Rasseneur and Souvarine are fixed in their ideas from the beginning to the end of the novel. Only Etienne evolves. In the *Ebauche* Rasseneur was originally destined for a more important role as representative of the International. His status as ex-miner, café owner and political leader is a typical one which owes a lot to Zola's meeting with Emile Basly during the strike at Anzin. Basly was in just such a position as Rasseneur, though further to the left in his politics. When Zola decided, however, to bring Etienne to the forefront of the novel, Rasseneur was inevitably pushed into the background.

Rasseneur is described in the *Ebauche* as a Possibilist, thus representing that relatively moderate wing of the working-class movement which was determined on piecemeal legislative reform and against any form of violent upheaval or revolution. Although the Possibilists of the Fédération du Parti des Travailleurs Socialistes de France still claimed connection with Marxist aims the quarrel over means with other members of the same party led to a split in 1882 whereby the more revolutionary members left to found the Parti Ouvrier Français under the leadership of Jules Guesde. The Possibilists were themselves split into differing tendencies, represented by Benoît Malon, Paul Brousse and others. This highly complex and shifting situation in the socialist movement is represented in Rasseneur in extremely simplified form. The ultimate vision of a socialist society is totally neglected and the political intention behind advances in legislation sought by the Possibilists is reduced to the level of a series of humble requests for kinder treatment. Rasseneur

> demandait seulement le possible aux patrons, sans exiger, comme tant d'autres, des choses trop dures à obtenir. (70)

Some vestige remains of Zola's intention of making Rasseneur the strike

leader in that at the end of Part I of the novel Rasseneur is mentioned as
being in correspondence with Pluchart in Lille, a role that devolves on
Etienne later on.

Rasseneur's politics are stated most clearly in the quarrel with Etienne
before the meeting at the Bon-Joyeux (IV, 4).

> La politique, le gouvernement, tout ça, je m'en fous! Ce que je désire,
> c'est que le mineur soit mieux traité. (227)

Although this is blurted out in the course of a dispute which causes both
Etienne and Rasseneur to exaggerate their own arguments, it does point
out clearly the direction in which Rasseneur's thought is tending.
Basically, he is separating the political from the social question, which
was one of the starting-points of Etienne's own thinking but which the
latter comes to reject as being a naïve view. Another resemblance with
Etienne which indicates a similarity in the original conception of their
roles is the personal element of ambition which each of them has. This
causes their differences of opinion in politics to be seen not so much in
ideological as in emotional terms. Each is jealous of the other's influence.
It is difficult to say for certain which comes first, ideas or temperament,
but Zola seems to be hinting that, given a common drive of ambition,
political ideologies are simply one way of crystallizing in public tempera-
mental differences, and where Etienne is a *rêveur/révolté* by temperament,
Rasseneur is 'un homme pratique' by temperament. At the height of the
riots Zola faintly suggests the possibility of treachery on Rasseneur's
part after his defeat at the Vandame forest meeting, and only removes
the doubt much later. There is an ambiguity in Rasseneur's conduct, as
there is in Etienne's. Rasseneur's existence is described as being based on
'camaraderie ambitieuse' (274). The ambitions of a workers' leader do
not prevent him from being able to lead, but do tend to cut him off in
many ways from the masses. Thus, Rasseneur is often described as
almost bourgeois in mentality, his 'bon sens d'homme établi' being
related to the fact that 'il s'enrichissait des colères qu'il avait peu à peu
soufflées au cœur de ses anciens camarades' (68). The last picture we
have of him is after he has saved Etienne from the wrath of the mob
and re-established his own influence:

> les deux hommes se regardèrent en silence. Tous deux haussèrent les
> épaules. Ils finirent par boire une chope ensemble. (425)

Behind the rediscovered fraternity between Rasseneur and Etienne (both have gone through the same cycle of acclaim and rejection) is a sense of complicity, in that they both realize the herd-like instincts of the masses. Both react here like old professionals in the struggle on behalf of the workers whom they control from time to time. More often, however, they sense their own impotence and display a despairing pity for the workers who represent a vast natural force which is ultimately not amenable to control, and certainly not to organization based on political ideology even in the attenuated form represented by Rasseneur.

Souvarine is at the other end of the spectrum of working-class political ideologies from Rasseneur. He is an intellectual and an anarchist. His Russian origins have been much studied,[8] and his presence in the novel seems to owe a good deal to Zola's conversations with his friend Turgenev and his reading of the latter's works, but also reflects the public interest in the populist campaigns of 1878–81 in Russia which culminated in the assassination of the Tsar Alexander II in 1881. Some of the details of Souvarine's earlier life in Russia (134) recall other attacks made by nihilists in the same period. Yet further details come from Laveleye's *Le Socialisme contemporain*.[9] While there is ample evidence to show Souvarine's Russian origins, his presence in the novel owes rather more to the middle-class fears of a Red terror brought about by the return to France in 1880 of the newly-amnestied political exiles of the Commune, and a series of anarchist-inspired riots and explosions in the early 1880s. This terror was already present at the time of the composition of *Germinal*, even though the anarchist campaign did not reach its height in France until the early 1890s.

Zola reflects this terror, but in an ambiguous fashion which combines it with a sense of fascination. The calm statements of the need for total destruction by this follower of Bakuninist ideas have much in common with the imaginative needs of Zola as novelist. The picture of 'la terre lavée par le sang, purifiée par l'incendie! . . .' (138) is certainly a part of the anarchist tradition but interestingly has also a great deal in common with the endings Zola provides for *La Débâcle* and *La Terre*. The transformation of the ideological standpoint into a personal Zolaesque vision is underlined when one hears the programme of the solemn, mystical anarchist in *Germinal* in the mouth of Maurice Levasseur, a debilitated bourgeois intellectual produced by the Second Empire in *La Débâcle*. The same vision is presented at the end of *La Terre* in terms which put

[8] See particularly the section on Souvarine in E. M. Grant, *op. cit.*, 71–83.

[9] For the general picture of anarchism in France at this period, see George Woodcock, *Anarchism* (Pelican books, 1963), 257–306.

the process on a cosmic level, where blood soaks the earth and fire is invoked, but where the earth and above all the eternal fertility of nature remain. By collapsing together such imaginatively similar scenes much of the purely political impact of *Germinal* is lost in favour of the cosmic vision of Zola.

Returning to the historical plane, it is evident that the background to the ideas exemplified by both Rasseneur and Souvarine is related to the early 1880s and is not an accurate picture of political influences and ideas as they stood in the France of the 1860s. Such touches as Zola does introduce in an attempt to point to an earlier period, for example Souvarine's prediction that 'Bakounine l'exterminateur' will shortly take over the International (231) which in fact happened in 1872 and was hardly foreseeable in 1865–6, serve only to confuse further the historical picture.

A subsidiary function of Souvarine, which is grafted on to his role as an anarchist intellectual, is to provide a rational explanation of the general economic situation, demonstrating that the mining company probably welcomes the strike given the current economic crisis. This picture, which Zola has taken from his documentary sources, is ascribed to Souvarine since: 'Lui seul avait l'intelligence assez déliée pour analyser la situation' (167). This economic analysis is completed by various speeches made by Deneulin.

Souvarine, like Etienne, walks out of the novel at the end. He has been responsible for the cataclysm and by the very enormity of his act has taken on mythical proportions. By his implied continuing presence in society and the total mystery of his ultimate destination he represents most clearly the figure intended to induce the shudder Zola wanted the middle-class reader to experience.

Etienne, on whom we have already concentrated from other angles, receives his socialist education from Rasseneur, Souvarine, Pluchart and the strike situation itself. He is the point at which the attitudes of others converge and who evolves under these influences from a naïve and instinctive sense of injustice to what Zola describes as a scientific and hardened attitude. At moments, and notably in his speech in the forest of Vandame, he leans towards Souvarine's anarchism, but in the end is described as having become a

> soldat raisonneur de la révolution, ayant déclaré la guerre à la société, telle qu'il la voyait et telle qu'il la condamnait. (496)

Such a picture seems to reinforce the overt intentions of Zola of making his hero at the end of his education a Marxist, or what he called in the *Ebauche* a 'collectiviste autoritaire'.

When one tries, however, to analyse the exact ideological position of Etienne, the edges of this seemingly clear-cut conclusion become blurred. The Marxist position is virtually equated by Zola with Darwinism, and, while both envisage life in terms of struggle and consequent change, it is clear that revolution is not the same thing as evolution. The novelist hovers between a conception of society perceived as an organic whole, developing by a process of natural selection, and a picture of class struggle within a divided capitalist society, and tends on the whole to telescope the political and the biological arguments. Etienne's education and consequent *embourgeoisement* have separated him from his class origins, and at the same time reinforced his hatred of the bourgeoisie. While determined to continue the struggle he is conscious that he may at any time be overtaken by the masses. He has already experienced being overtaken by events during the rioting from mine to mine, has already suffered from the volatility of the emotions of the masses at the end of the strike, and though he is still willing, indeed totally committed, to defending them as a class, he now also partly fears them as representing a force of nature which will possibly devour him.

One could draw a very pessimistic picture of the objective situation of the miners at the end of the strike. The strike has been crushed, the power of capital has been increased, the large company swallowing up the small independent capitalist. The miners have been driven back to work on the company's terms, a class traitor like Pierron has been promoted, strikers have been killed, the strike fund is exhausted, the embryo union organization has collapsed, Etienne and Souvarine leave the community. The mining company finally has tided itself over a period of general industrial crisis on the cheap.

In the last pages of the novel, however, Zola sets up against this picture images of spring and germination, the working class taking power one day when the grain is ripe. This optimism which breaks through the prevailing atmosphere of the novel is not simply a political prediction, but a deep-seated need in Zola himself. The crushing blackness of the general situation, established by observation and analysis, is counterbalanced by a poem of faith in the future. A very similar equation had been used in *La Joie de vivre*, where a novel of physical pain and moral suffering agonizingly delineated gives way to an affirmation of happiness in life, hope in spite of everything, and a condemnation of pessimism. What Zola refrains from showing, or perhaps is even incapable of showing, is how the progression is to be made, what means employed. Zola says that the agents of the revolution will be the working class. La Maheude's final attitude, however, is significant of Zola's ambiguity over distinguishing the means available:

> Elle était revenue à son calme de femme raisonnable, elle jugeait très sagement les choses. Ça ne porterait pas chance aux bourgeois, d'avoir tué tant de pauvres gens. Bien sûr qu'ils en seraient punis un jour, car tout se paie. On n'aurait pas même besoin de s'en mêler, la boutique sauterait seule, les soldats tireraient sur les patrons, comme ils avaient tiré sur les ouvriers. Et, dans sa résignation séculaire, dans cette hérédité de discipline qui la courbait de nouveau, un travail s'était ainsi fait, la certitude que l'injustice ne pouvait durer davantage, et que, s'il n'y avait plus de bon Dieu il en repousserait un autre, pour venger les misérables. (493–4)

This fatalism, combined with the belief in the return of a sort of political Messiah (this latter is a permanent feature of the strikers' mentality; they are often described also as thinking and behaving like members of the early Christian church) is placed side by side with Etienne's final observations of the miners 'les dents serrées de colère, le cœur gonflé de haine . . .' (489) and the emotional handshake with le père Mouque:

> une poignée de main . . . la même que celle des autres, longue, chaude de colère rentrée, frémissante des rébellions futures. (491)

Etienne's own conclusions are an amalgam of the emotional, the gradualist and the revolutionary. He dreams of regenerating the universe by glorifying the workers, and, while retaining his belief in day to day progress brought about by Parliaments and the legal process, envisages the day when the workers will simply take power and be the masters. To the very end he is unable to achieve a synthesis between the dream of one day waking up in the realm of truth and justice and his observations of class hatred and desire for vengeance to which he also gives his full support.

The ideological debate within the working-class movement is reflected by Zola, but most often in terms of conflict between personalities or even, in the case of Etienne, within the personality itself. Etienne's stance is ambiguous, moving freely across the range that goes from sentimental dreams of utopia to various theories of socialism and the temptations of anarchism. By describing Etienne's ideological education as completed at the end of *Germinal* Zola is brushing the loose ends of his socialism under the carpet, in an attempt to provide an invigorating vision of the future. The political education has many of the overtones of a moral conquest. It is paralleled by the sexual education which has also provided an experience which has ended in failure in the short term but which has succeeded in liberating Etienne's virility and sense of self. The intolerable tensions implicit in politics and sexuality, which have their origins in the fascinated observation of social and sexual realities, are both resolved by a leap into a future of dreams and by the abandonment of the circumscribed *milieu* in which the tensions had their origins.

## The bourgeois world and its presentation

Although one of the major themes of *Germinal* is the struggle between capital and labour, Zola's imagination drew him increasingly towards the presentation of the narrative from the working-class viewpoint. The struggle in which he had intended to allot equal shares to each side comes down strongly on the side of the miners. The study of the bourgeois viewpoint thus becomes semi-occluded, and in some ways a re-run of themes dealt with more fully in the bourgeois novels of the series.

Zola carves a gulf between the two classes. There are a few NCO-type figures like the overmen Dansaert or Richomme, the one unsympathetic, the other sympathetic, and the cameo of le père Quandieu. Another intermediary figure is Maigrat. But this handful has to serve to designate the whole class of foremen, clerks, small shopkeepers, schoolteachers, and others, who might normally be expected to hold the middle ground between the two classes in Montsou, for Zola is interested not in showing the subtle gradations of a complex social hierarchy, but in affecting the reader in the strongest possible way by underlining differences. He expresses this clearly in the *Ebauche*:

> Pour obtenir un gros effet, il faut que les oppositions soient nettes et poussées au summum de l'intensité possible.

One or two figures, Pierron and Chaval for example, are shown in the process of moving from one group to the other, but they emerge clearly as class traitors.

This technique of introducing a major cleavage between the two classes is part of the much broader and still deliberate technique of concentration of effect. Much has been rightly made of Zola's vast canvases and his epic effects, but it is perhaps less obvious that he achieves this with great economy. Although there are more than fifty named characters in this novel, over half of them are introduced to the reader in the first three chapters of Part I. After the opening chapter of Part II the only major character still to be presented is Souvarine. All the others are purely episodic. This relatively rapid introduction of the full cast, described quickly in broad outlines, allows Zola to spread himself on establishing the weight of the *milieu* in which the figures will evolve, and to concentrate many of his effects there.

Just as Zola eliminates as many as possible of the intermediate figures in the social hierarchy, so also he isolates Montsou and its *corons* as much as possible from the outside world. The vast plains planted with corn and sugar-beet do not serve simply as a photograph of reality, even less as a symbol of openness and freedom as in the frontier myth in many American novels, but fulfil the function of cutting off the world of *Germinal* from the rest of society. They isolate the community and thrust it in on itself. Slight touches here and there indicate that there are other industries in and around Montsou, but their influence on the miners is negligible. Zola also eliminated electoral scenes he had originally planned, and reduced to virtually nil the references to the Parisian end of the mining company. Similarly, one has singularly little impression that Montsou is a town and is a little surprised to find towards the end of the novel a scene set in a 'faubourg industriel' (392), implying the presence elsewhere of a town centre. The people who fill it are barely alluded to—an anonymous *notaire* is mentioned (336) and on the same page a public reaction to the miners' march is sketched—'les habitants s'agitaient, affolés de panique'—but that is all. At the level of the simplest detail one might presume, too, that in the early days of the strike Maheu sells the trout he catches to a member of the bourgeoisie, but Zola does not encourage the reader to think in terms of possible links between the classes. There is no mention either of the sort of odd-jobbing that is one of the natural resources of the worker during a strike. All this leaves those characters who are discussed in detail to face each other across the gulf of class with the maximum effect of contrast.

The three bourgeois families are clearly chosen to embody different aspects of the capitalist side of the social system: Hennebeau, the salaried manager, Deneulin, the small-scale independent capitalist, and Grégoire, the *rentier*. In spite of this, all of them have in common a clear interest in the maintenance of the *status quo*. This class interest is revealed and sustained typically around the dining table and in an over-heated atmosphere. The antithesis between the warmth, comfort and self-indulgence of the bourgeois world and the chill, harsh and poverty-striken environment of the working class is complete.

The Grégoire family functions as a complete contrast to the Maheu family. Where the Maheus have a large number of pale and sickly children, the Grégoires have a solitary pink-faced child bursting with health. The Grégoires' day begins at 9 a.m. or even later for Cécile, who is watched over tenderly by the family and servants and allowed to sleep on in the mornings. Whereas the Maheus get up in stress and confusion (83–4) the Grégoire household is permanently calm. Catherine Maheu rises at 4 a.m., even though desperately tired. It is she who gets things moving, and prepares a breakfast of coffee made from already used grounds, while the Grégoires have the servants serve rich breakfast chocolate and freshly-baked *brioche*. The overheated and sickeningly sentimental family atmosphere of the Grégoires' contrasts again with the atmosphere at the Maheus' where most reactions are dulled by exhaustion, poverty and hunger. The ogre of capitalism or 'dieu repu' as it is perceived by the workers becomes from the Grégoires' side of the fence

> comme une divinité à eux, que leur égoïsme entourait d'un culte, la bienfaitrice du foyer, les berçant dans leur grand lit de paresse, les engraissant à leur table gourmande. (78)

The irony is extended by play on a stock phrase when the Grégoires describe their house as 'la maison du bon Dieu' (90).

The systematic parallels between the two families are underlined by their common link with the mine which goes back through exactly the same number of generations on each side to its foundation. Each family has its view of history dating from the setting up of the company. Bonnemort's picture of Maheu history is given in the introductory chapter to Part I, and is paralleled by Grégoire history in the introductory chapter to Part II. The two histories come together in their current representatives when la Maheude goes to La Piolaine to ask for money. The Grégoires react in what they conceive to be a charitable way, full of a sense of pity accompanied by just a touch of unease which is quickly suppressed. Their thoughts and speech represent bourgeois morality in its purest form. First is the notion that it is they who have lessons to teach the workers, and then the whole litany of reproaches: the workers have too many children, drink too much, live virtually rent-free and with free coal. The Grégoires are willing to give clothing, but never money. Their cosy little world is utterly untouched by that of the miners. The word 'strike' for Cécile means pleasurable recollections of charity visits to the poor.

Zola has treated them in a richly ironic way, and was to use the same technique in portraying M. and Mme Charles Badeuil in *La Terre* where a calm bourgeois *rentier* existence drifts on ignoring the terrible passions at play beyond the walls of their property. Their sentimental morality and the good convent education given to their granddaughter hides the fact that the family wealth was gained originally by good management of a brothel in Chartres. In the final part of *Germinal* however, Zola roughly tips the Grégoire family out of the cloud-cuckoo-land they inhabit, and has Cécile strangled by Bonnemort,[10] thereby abandoning the ironic presentation in favour of the symbolic, the future of the *rentier* class being eliminated by the blind impulse of the ancestral miner.

The picture of the Hennebeau household repeats the bourgeois motifs of an overheated atmosphere, the life centred round the dining table, comfort and self-indulgence. Another element is introduced, however, which takes up ideas more fully exploited earlier in the Rougon-Macquart series. The sexual life of Hennebeau recalls several of Zola's pictures of bourgeois sexual *mores* from *La Curée* to *Pot-Bouille*. The earlier novels of the Rougon-Macquart series had included as a dominant element the satire of the bourgeoisie in tones which in spite of variations evoke essentially a sense of disgust, symbolized by the last line of *Le Ventre de Paris*: 'Quels gredins que les honnêtes gens!' Zola owed much of his reputation for obscenity to the fact that these earlier novels had pointed out in great detail the contrast between a pure, honest-dealing and correct appearance and a disgusting, humiliating and often tormented reality in bourgeois existence. The theme is restated in the case of Hennebeau by using the contrast between his calm attitude in public, reinforced by the repeated mention of his tightly-buttoned coat and stiff military bearing, and the total wreck of his private life. Zola shows how the conquest of a prominent position in the bourgeois hierarchy is gained at the expense of natural or instinctual behaviour. In this context Hennebeau is exemplary, representing that part of the bourgeoisie which is still advancing, whereas the Grégoires represent attitudes in process of fossilization—their history coming to a stop with the murder of Cécile—and Deneulin is defeated as an individual and reabsorbed into the system at a lower level. It is true that Zola presents Hennebeau

[10] Zola at first hesitated whether to have Cécile conclude her marriage with Négrel. See E. M. Grant, 'Marriage or murder: Zola's hesitations concerning Cécile Grégoire', *French Studies* (1961), 41-6.

in a tragic light when, after the discovery of his wife's infidelity, he watches the miners crying for bread, and wishes he could be one of them rather than endure the misery of his personal existence (V, 5). But while this tragedy is presented with all the flourishes of bourgeois rhetoric, and while Hennebeau dreams of moving from the artificial world of the bourgeoisie to the natural world of the miners in an attempt to diminish the 'éternelle douleur', the 'souffrance inassouvie des passions' (338), he never makes a gesture in that direction, and in fact has just dispatched orders for troops to set in motion the repression of the strike. This implied criticism is extended to Mme Hennebeau. She certainly indulges her passionate and sensual nature but has not the liberty of instinct Zola accords to the working class, for her use of passions is perverse. Her affair with Négrel is quasi-incestuous, being described most often in terms of a mother and son relationship, and is an echo of the situation between Renée Saccard and her stepson Maxime in *La Curée*, even down to the description of the disordered, scent-laden, hothouse atmosphere of love.

A curious problem arises from this class interpretation of passions suggested by Zola, in which the bourgeoisie is equated with either a sterile, blocked or perverse emotional life and the proletariat used as a metaphor for emotional freedom, naturalness and fertility, a theme to be later much dwelt upon by D. H. Lawrence and which still persists in contemporary literature. This relatively clear picture is confused by the attribution to the proletarian Etienne of a blocked emotional life similar to Hennebeau's, which effectively poses the problem independently of the class structure. Etienne eventually escapes, however, by planting his seed in the womb of Catherine. This act is clearly intended to be life-giving and liberating, and although the idea of Etienne being moved by the thought that Catherine had perhaps been made pregnant in the minutes before she died is superficially grotesque given the circumstances, the need to express hope via fertility is so strong as to override such considerations, and is linked emotionally with the notion of the miners becoming the seed of the future revolution. Zola has, therefore, saved Etienne from the trap of frustrated passions to which both he and the bourgeoisie were originally subject. Etienne escapes by the gift of natural love which allows the personal problem to rejoin the social problem in an expression of faith in the future of the liberated individual and a class. This contrasts completely with the final image of Hennebeau, his wife and Négrel, condemned to continue their hideous charade, Hennebeau even finding a virtue in Cécile having been strangled:

Ce malheur arrangeait tout, il préférait garder son neveu, dans la crainte de son cocher. (467)

This total moral blindness of the bourgeoisie, provided appearances are kept up, is achieved by an ability to shut out what is screamingly obvious, as in the scene where Mme Hennebeau shows a bourgeois couple round the *coron* (II, 3). They are first shown la Pierronne's clean and well-kept house to the accompaniment of a running commentary from the other miners' wives: 'Si c'était propre dessus, ce n'était guère propre dessous.' It is natural here that the bourgeois visitors should not realize the hidden truths behind the cleanness, for it is the household of a social climber aping the behaviour of the bourgeoisie. When, however, they visit la Maheude's house, smell the odour of poverty, see the children with their enlarged heads, observe Alzire with her hunchback, and Bonnemort ashen-looking and racked by coughing fits, their first reaction is the same as the Grégoires': 'une compassion pleine de malaise'. But they are also able to pass without transition to the mouthing of commonplaces:

> . . . mœurs patriarcales, tous heureux et bien portants comme vous voyez, un endroit où vous devriez venir vous refaire un peu, à cause du bon air et de la tranquillité.—C'est merveilleux, merveilleux! cria le monsieur, dans un élan final d'enthousiasme.

This fairly gross form of irony underlines Zola's deliberate intention of exposing not just the problem of relations between classes but the scandal of the wilful ignorance of the bourgeoisie.

The most sympathetic treatment of a member of this class is that accorded to Deneulin. With his hard-working but quick-tempered approach to life, this enterprising engineer with the air of a cavalry officer invests all his wealth in modernizing his mine which is insufficiently capitalized to stand the strain of the economic crisis. This side of him can be seen as a portrait of Zola's own father, ex-officer in the artillery and civil engineer who died when Zola was not quite seven, leaving behind an uncompleted scheme for constructing a canal to provide the city of Aix with fresh water, which had taken up all his capital and left his widow and young son virtually penniless. Hence the stress on Deneulin's paternalism, addressing his workers as 'mes enfants', and Zola's provision of a tender picture of reciprocated love between him and his daughters. Significantly, it is Deneulin who is in charge of the reconstruction of the *canal* after the flooding of Le Voreux.

All this does not prevent him adopting class attitudes however, when under stress. He regrets not having asked for armed police to guard his pit, and his last cry before Jean-Bart is attacked is 'Tas de bandits, vous verrez ça, quand nous serons redevenus les plus forts!' (307). This extreme situation has led him to speak like all the other bourgeois characters, but a little reflection brings him back closer to his earlier more sympathetic attitudes, and he is able to see the situation with a sort of stoicism:

> . . . il sentait la complicité de tous, une faute générale, séculaire. Des brutes sans doute, mais des brutes qui ne savaient pas lire et qui crevaient de faim. (312)

This feeling of compassion is the closest approach bourgeois ideology can make to the working class, without calling into question the existence of the bourgeoisie as a class. There has been 'faute', certainly, but it is 'générale, séculaire'. It is not seen by the bourgeoisie as the product of a system, but has instead all the overtones of Fate.

## The working-class world

Recent critics, reacting against the simplified view of Zola as a sociological novelist passing from subject to subject in his attempt to provide a panorama of the society of the Second Empire, have tended to play down the overt subjects of his works, preferring to stress formal or structural elements or to analyse the nature of his vision. This has given rise to a complex Zola and a Zola of complexes. Auguste Dezalay, for example, prefers to

> insister sur la nécessité parfois de décrypter, ou de déchiffrer, chez Zola, une sorte de langage codé, sous l'apparence d'un discours facile et rassurant pour le lecteur.[11]

Jean Borie, working from a Freudian standpoint, rejects the notion of Zola's works being a collection of subjects, and finds in them

> non pas un éparpillement documentaire, mais un seul sujet sans cesse reprise . . .[12]

an obsession with the functions of the body and its 'scandalous' secrets, and a series of searches for a cure. It seems worthwhile, though, to try and appreciate for a moment the interest of Zola's picture of the working-

[11] Auguste Dezalay, *Lectures de Zola* (Colin, 1973), 252.
[12] J. Borie, *op. cit.*, 22.

class world of the miners on its own terms, before seeing it as a metaphor
or a sign for something else. We shall ignore the study of working-class
sexual habits, as the instinct itself is common to all classes and we have
already mentioned the subject in connection with the psychology of
Etienne and bourgeois morality. Let us simply repeat that, broadly
speaking, Zola contrasts the natural and uninhibited behaviour of the
working class (Etienne excepted) with the artificial, frustrated or perverse behaviour of the bourgeoisie. Natural behaviour, however, seems
to imply relationships with one partner only, be it before or after marriage. Those women breaking the single partner bond are condemned,
and Catherine sees the possibility of changing partners as the beginning
of the slippery slope that will lead her to the brothels in Lille. The only
figures who escape this rule are la Mouquette and la veuve Désir who
seem excused on grounds of superabundant sexual needs!

Many things have changed in the miner's life since Zola's day, but
much has remained the same. A quick reading of newspaper articles at
the beginning of 1974 shows journalists carrying out inquiries in mining
areas and reporting details of mining life which might just as well have
been lifted from Zola a century ago: reduced pay for miners forced to
do surface work after illness contracted underground, constant fires
raging underground in shut-off sections of a pit, miners after their shift
using a pint of beer to clear the coaldust from their throats, feelings of
melancholy but determined resignation on the eve of a strike, and so on.
Although the miner's pick has given way to modern machinery,
although women and children are no longer found down the mines
and the zinc tub in front of the fire has been replaced by pithead baths,
the filth, darkness, dampness, extremes of temperature and danger still
remain, as do the illnesses and injuries. It is not merely the latter aspects
of the life which interest Zola—though they do interest him and move
him to pity that men should be subject to such conditions in their daily
work—but also its elemental nature, notions of being buried alive in
the bowels of the earth and the consequent terrors induced in men, and
so on. Zola has, of course, fused the two aspects in *Germinal*, and we
have already seen how Etienne tries to reach a stability or a synthesis in
his relating of the outside world to the terrors within himself.

The sheer mass of detail, however, in the opening parts of the novel
is clearly intended to show, and does show, the external aspects of the
existence of the miners. It is here that Zola has introduced most systematically the material acquired during his visit to Anzin. Part I is structured
around the picture of the miner's working day from the painful waking

up in the morning to the exhausted silence of the evening. Part I, ch. 2, starts with a description of the Maheu family and their house, which is intended to be typical of the whole village. Indeed, Zola originally wished to underline the fact by giving them the name Durand, whose equivalent in Britain would be Smith or Jones. The next chapter focuses on the mine, the pithead area and the journey to work underground. While Chapter 2 takes the family group as a unifying element, Chapter 3 is largely based on the work group. Zola introduces his documentary material in very brief doses of a line or two each. Thus, his description of miners' dress (20), the miners' sandwich or 'le briquet' (24), the miners' crouch (46), or a quick summary of attitudes in the five or six lines on the new laws about employment of women (31). The accumulation of such details is not simply to serve as a 'picturesque' background, but to provide an implicit explanation of the influence of work and surroundings on human beings. Other details, such as the interior of the various houses, describe the imprint made by human beings on their surroundings. This aspect of *Germinal*, although not new as a technique in the novel—Balzac is the most obvious predecessor of Zola in this—is important, and cannot be excluded from any study of the 'vision' of Zola, simply because the obsessional or the hallucinatory in his works is more obviously striking to the modern reader.

Zola stresses the extreme poverty of the miners and their hand-to-mouth existence, giving on two occasions a breakdown of the Maheu family's earnings (22 and 173). The great inadequacy of their diet is obvious even before the strike breaks out. A disastrous pay-day is the starting point of the strike, although its actual cause, as with most strikes, is attributable to a whole complex of reasons. Zola is explicit about the workers' pay: 3 francs a day for a face worker, 2 francs a day for a female underground worker and male surface worker, 1 franc a day for a child worker, all this only for the days actually worked, and with deductions for bad work or dirty coal. He articulates less in economic terms how the miners actually manage to exist during the strike which lasts from mid-December until it begins to collapse at the end of February or beginning of March, for the mid-December pay of 50 francs for the Maheu family is already represented as 'la mort bientôt' (175). What Zola has chosen to do is to set off the strike in a paroxysm of anger and poverty. Having pitched the tone so high at the outset, he cannot continue it in purely economic terms—there is virtually no strike fund, a solid family like the Maheus have already exhausted their credit at the grocer's, debts are still being paid off from an earlier strike—and marks the progress of time and the effects of the strike in human and pictorial terms. This is gradated from pictures of the inert machinery to increasing cold, and hunger. An old woman dies, women start roaming the streets driven out by hunger. Rioting begins. Alzire dies of malnutrition in a dead world of cold, snow and ice. Although Zola suggests one or two means of obtaining money—selling the furniture, for example—it seems unlikely that this would have supported a large family like the Maheus over such a period. What he does instead is to whip the reader's senses in order to maintain the cumulative effect of the misery. The energy of the narrative covers the fact that he has said 'déjà tout manquait' (216) at the end of December, 'les corons agonisaient d'heure en heure . . . toute ressource manqua . . . sans pain et sans feu . . .' (241-2) in the early days of January, and still the strike continues until at least late February. This constant state of extreme misery is punctuated by a series of acts of extreme violence, and by scenes such as the successive descriptions of the interior of the Maheus' house displaying each time greater poverty. By cross-currents such as this Zola produces the impression of increasing tension and misery in a situation which has already been set off at a very high level.

Although the miners' world is dominated by work, cold and hunger, Zola allows occasional scenes to suggest a life that could be normal if the oppressive circumstances were lifted. These scenes could be grouped roughly under the heading of popular culture. They cover religion, history and play. The religion has nothing to do with the faith propagated by the abbé Joire, nor even with the Christian socialism put forward by the abbé Ranvier, but is an orally transmitted set of legends based on figures of retribution lurking in the mines. Catherine is shown as especially sensitive to these beliefs, but they affect all the miners in some degree: 'gardant la peur secrète des revenants de la fosse, mais s'égayant du ciel vide' (160). This religious sense sometimes takes on overtones of the early Christian Church however, particularly in the political discussions, as in the meeting in the forest of Vandame.[13]

Bonnemort passes on the historical culture of the working class, and is shown in some ways as embodying it. This historical sense does not die as he fades into senility, la Maheude being shown as the likely inheritor of this knowledge. She already has her own recollections of

[13] It has been said that the scene is based on the politico-religious meeting in the woods in Balzac's *Les Chouans*. One could equally well trace it to the nocturnal harangue of the priestess Velléda to the Gauls in Chateaubriand's *Les Martyrs*, Book 9.

the 1848 Revolution (219) to add to Bonnemort's history. Zola repeats this mixture of folk religion and history in *La Terre*, revealing it during a *veillée* in winter, but this time of course seen through peasants' eyes.

The treatment of working-class relaxations suggests the existence of a living culture which has nothing to do with bourgeois culture and relaxations. The scene of the miners' *ducasse* (III, 2) concentrates this study, with its fairground atmosphere, the birdsong contests, cock-fighting, skittles and long pub-crawls. To this one can add the description of the primitive game of golf between Zacharie and Mouquet (264–6). What is common to the description of the *ducasse* and the *partie de crosse* is the whirlwind atmosphere in which Zola catches them up. This reflects not merely the semi-drunken state in which these pleasures are taken but also the increasingly desperate sense of snatching at a pleasure which can only be temporary and only sustained by whipping the senses into virtual oblivion. One can symbolize it by Levaque calling for more beer towards the end of the day of the *ducasse*

> attendri de voir qu'on était tous là, en famille . . . —Nom de Dieu! on ne s'amuse pas si souvent! gueulait-il. (153)

## Beyond naturalism

Zola conceived *Germinal* as a drama of violent contrasts. One of them is the scandal of the misery of the present put against the dream of a shining world that might be. Zola has infinite faith in the idea that humanity will progress from the one to the other. In spite of his suggestions towards a political solution, he is not clear how this change can be brought about and creates the myth of the seed planted in the soil of the present, flourishing and being harvested in the future. The conflict between the reality and the dream is thus resolved in poetic myth.

Before this germination, however, the mine, a monster in itself, has been the scene of cosmic conflict where all the elements, earth, air, fire and water, have been exploited by Zola. The various forms of physical death or mental torture are represented by presences and monsters. For these latter Zola draws on the resources provided by Greek, biblical and Celtic mythology for many of his figures of speech.[14] One of the keys to his use of these mythologies is in his assimilation of the life underground to a life in the underworld, the miners becoming damned

[14] For a detailed examination of one aspect of this subject, see Philip D. Walker, 'Prophetic myths in Zola', *P.M.L.A.* (1959), 444–52.

creatures in hell. All the associations of hell and hell-fire are called upon. Their influence covers the specific burning hell of Le Tartaret underground. The name evokes the Greek Tartarus, the abyss in which the Titans were confined. Zola does not pursue these associations, however, preferring the biblical connotations of the destruction of the city of Sodom and the eternal torments of hell-fire (289 and 291–2). These notions of fire invade even the world above ground, starting with simple denomination as in the case of *Le Volcan*, the name of a bar, or la Roussie (123), the name of a female miner of long ago, and being elaborated in la Brûlé, a wild figure scorched into revolt by the mine, who becomes a witch in the attack on Jean-Bart, shrieking 'Faut renverser les feux! aux chaudières!' egging on the women

> toutes sanglantes dans le reflet d'incendie, suantes et échevelées de cette cuisine de sabbat. (308–9)

The damned souls are pursued not only by fire but also by flood. The sabotage of the mine-shaft at the level of an underground lake and consequent flooding of the workings is transformed by Zola into an immense cataclysmic scene. References are made to drowned cities. In spite of the miners trapped below, the scene is represented in terms of a spectacle. The watching miners are fascinated by the cosmic forces at work and end by fleeing in terror. In the actual description of the collapse of the pit (448–51), Zola has eliminated any direct feeling of pity for the trapped miners or sense of revenge on the mining company, concentrating all his effects instead on the animate natural forces at play. In such a scheme human beings are irrelevant, for the enormity of the spectacle witnessed is but one drama contained within a vaster one yet:

> Jusqu'où devait-on fuir, pour être à l'abri, dans cette fin de jour abominable, sous cette nuée de plomb, qui elle aussi semblait vouloir écraser le monde? (452)

A whole chain of images of the earth squeezing, squashing, flattening the miners below ground is here repeated above ground level. Even in the open air the miners are subject to these huge commotions, being squeezed below the weight of the sky and with the earth splitting, cracking and being engulfed below them. The terror of humanity becomes then the basic fear of no longer existing, and the gnawing worry that human existence or non-existence seen in this cosmic perspective is perhaps almost of no import anyhow. The result is a sense of pity at human fate. The image of Maheu at the coalface:

entre les deux roches, ainsi qu'un puceron pris entre deux feuillets
d'un livre, sous la menace d'un aplatissement complet (41)

can stand as a typical statement of this situation. At this level Zola is
writing an evolutionary epic, in which the role of humanity is negligible.
This sort of conclusion throws doubt on the validity of the optimistic
ending to the novel, and indeed on the whole theme of germination and
*Germinal* as a political novel. Zola plays on the ambiguity and tensions
between these two conclusions, the one pessimistic, the other optimistic,
and succeeds in transforming the former into the latter by reversing the
connotations of images. For example, while the earth is shown normally
as digesting its regular ration of human flesh in its belly, these images of
the various stages of digestion are transformed into notions of germination or gestation. The belly of the earth turns in the end from a stomach
into a womb, the word 'ventre' covering both meanings. Similar are the
connotations of mud and filth (as opposed to the simple images of
blackness and whiteness in the earlier parts of the novel) which dominate
the opening of Part VI, ch. 4, symbolizing at this stage misery and
desolation. This picture is continued at the moment of the collapse of
Le Voreux, one of the final statements being 'un lac d'eau boueuse
occupa la place où était naguère le Voreux . . .' (452). Out of this drama
of filth and degradation, we have reached a point where the disgust
has drained away, leaving a sense of moral punishment, which in its
turn gives way at the end of the last chapter to images of the rich and
fertile earth, where the liquid element is now sap, and life. Such trans-
formations are not specific to *Germinal*. In *La Terre*, too, Zola shows
human and animal excrement being transformed from disgusting faecal
muck to solemn and richly fertile manure.

This mythology of cosmic struggle and renewal contains within it
the similar human struggle of misery, death and promise of renewal.
It is at this level that the political and psychological dramas take place,
each producing its own mythology. The political aspects have perhaps
been sufficiently discussed above, except for the key scenes of the raging
mass of miners (V, 3–6) which provide the dramatic centre of the novel.
Here Zola draws on a simplified mythology of the French Revolution
to underline his meaning, with mouths (not whole people) singing the
*Marseillaise*, an axe-blade transformed into the blade of the guillotine,
repeated cries for bread and a blood-red light bathing the whole
spectacle (333–5). This particular scene, drawing on what is virtually
a folk-memory of the Revolution, illuminates that other aspect of

the title of the novel which refers to the day of 12 Germinal in the third year of the Republican era (1 April 1795) when, in protest at reactionary measures taken since the fall of Robespierre, the Convention was invaded by Parisians demanding bread and a return to the more revolutionary constitution of 1793. The title thus refers not only to the idea of springtime but also to the French Revolution and gives full weight to both of the terms used by Zola when he described his novel as representing 'un avril révolutionnaire'.[15] This revolutionary theme is linked by Zola to that of instinctual behaviour. At the same time as he is appealing to revolutionary mythology he is also describing a progressive invasion of animal-like instincts which displace individual behaviour in the scenes of riot. The masses gallop over the countryside. The frequent repetition of the word gallop in Germinal signifies most often the idea of a wild, natural, virile but blind force driving the miners on. At the same time, under extreme pressure human beings are not only physically dislocated by Zola, becoming limbs, eyes, feet, and so on, indistinguishable except as a mass, but also revert to a primitive, pre-human shape, essentially wolf-like. The substance of such a deformation is treated most fully in La Bête humaine, but is already outlined in Germinal, where the 'faces placides des houilleurs de Montsou' become 'mâchoires de bêtes fauves' (334). Come the revolution, the men 'auraient ces mâchoires de loups, ouvertes pour mordre' (334). The moral ambiguity of such a mytholigical anthropology is evident. For how can one approve an event which, while supposedly liberating, implies a regression to the caveman or earlier species? It seems that Zola is in fact again mediating the bourgeois 'frisson d'horreur' in such images, while stressing the inevitability of such a process. This inevitability links with another series of images where the mass of miners becomes a river bursting its banks, swelling and overflowing the countryside, an unstoppable torrent in full flood.

This relative dehumanizing of human beings, particularly at moments of high tension or when seen in the mass, is paralleled by the relative humanizing of inanimate objects, such as the mine and pithead machinery. Both the sexual symbolism apparent in the description of the machine and the fascination and terror in the face of the instincts and appetite of the mine, are figures of a prevailing spirit moving the universe as a whole which includes the procreative urge as well as the urge to kill, but which turns in Germinal on the nodal image of appetite.

[15] In a letter to Van Santen Kolff, dated 6 October 1889.

The mine is repeatedly described as voracious, swallowing its daily ration of miners (for example 28-9). The revolutionary cries for bread represent 'le cri du ventre' (339), and the revolution may be brought about 'en se mangeant les uns les autres' (137). Maheu's appetite is described in the same terms as that of the mine: '(il) englouti(t) la pâtée' (108), 'attaqua le fromage de cochon' (109), the children watch the meat 's'engouffrer dans la bouche' (109). These expressions are fairly banal, but acquire special resonance when put alongside all the other examples of voracious eating. The terminology is extended, for example, to the sex act with la Maheude which her husband calls 'prendre son dessert' (112-13). The whole history of the nineteenth century is that of a gross banquet laid out for the bourgeoisie alone:

> c'étaient les bourgeois qui s'engraissaient depuis 89, si goulûment, qu'ils ne . . . laissaient même pas le fond des plats à torcher. (137)

This picture is systematically repeated whenever the bourgeoisie is gathered together. The omnipresence of these images brings back to life even stock expressions as when Etienne is described as 'dévoré surtout du besoin de savoir' (138), and his reading as 'mal digérée' (157). The conflict between Etienne and Chaval is consistently presented in terms of appetite: 'il fallait que l'un des deux mangeât l'autre' (221), including the extreme 'leurs yeux se mangeaient' (440). Etienne's killing of Chaval is 'un appétit enfin satisfait' (478). The list could be almost endlessly prolonged, but for Zola it is clear that the life force is essentially an appetite, a voracious hunger. Death is not eating. Such imagery is not merely the manifestation of Zola's notions of 'physiological' man, but expresses the way in which human biology links with the evolution of nature as a whole. While this evolution is progressive and leads in the end to happiness, Zola nevertheless remains as creative novelist much more in the realm of the hell-fire preacher playing on fears, terror, disgust, the plagues and afflictions of the world. It is this which gives such extraordinary power to his oppressive evocations of cold, hunger, sickness, death, collapse and catastrophe.

## Conclusion

At the time of the publication of *Germinal* Zola was widely known, notorious some would say; his literary influence, though hotly contested, was enormous, and was for many inseparable from his long history as a journalist and especially as a fighting journalist. His novels were not regarded simply as artefacts interesting mainly to the literary world, but increasingly as public statements by a polemicist. Thus, for many readers *Germinal* is an example of committed literature, in spite of Zola's efforts at impartiality and the attitudes we have shown to be often ambiguous. The picture of miners' delegations at Zola's funeral crying 'Germinal! Germinal!', the recent account[16] by Jean-Pierre Chabrol of *Germinal* forming, with Hugo's *Les Misérables* and the Bible, part of the folk-lore of the mining and peasant communities of the Cévennes, demonstrate clearly how far this work has overflowed the boundaries of readership and influence granted normally to works of art. However much we may wish to modify this popular appreciation, such a framework must necessarily form a part of the understanding of the novel.

Zola himself would not automatically have refused the suggestion that *Germinal* is a piece of committed literature, but would have limited it to the idea of provoking a reaction to a social problem and its implications rather than to providing specific solutions. His aesthetic stance as a naturalist novelist expounding the facts of a given situation with an attempt at what he conceived to be scientific impartiality, while not necessarily excluding the drawing of conclusions, does at least inhibit him from turning the work into a propaganda exercise.

While it is clear that the explicit subject of the novel is the struggle between capital and labour placed in the stylized battle situation of a strike, it is equally clear that the resulting composition is far from being simply that. The recurrence of a good number of scenes and themes found in Zola's other works shows the permanence of certain traits, certain situations repeated obsessively, so that the exposition of a strike in the pits becomes also the occasion for a personal drama in Zola's mind. The resulting tensions and ambiguities between the 'public' and the 'private' dramas go a long way to giving this novel its particular tone.

Ultimately, however, both these aspects of the novel are subsumed into a cosmic drama of life and death, shot through with passion. At this level, while not denying the importance of either the individual or the group, Zola sees his subject in mythological terms, in which all nature is animate and human struggles are but one factor in the continuation of the life-force. The evolution and, it may be, the progress of humanity is a by-product. Teeming and swarming may simply be

[16] In *Cahiers naturalistes* 36 (1968), 117–22.

instinctive reactions by humans to these huge stresses, and pity at such a fate the most dignified emotional response after the initial terror of realization. Thus we have a novel moving freely from the day-to-day to a time-scale suggesting millennia, from the picture of the Maheu family's clogs lined up under the sideboard to the eternal forces of nature.

# Bibliographical Note

The edition to which reference is made in the text is that of the widely available Le Livre de poche. The best critical edition is that contained in volume 3 of the 5-volume Gallimard, N.R.F., Bibliothèque de la Pléiade edition of *Les Rougon-Macquart*, which has a full description of the Bibliothèque nationale MS of *Germinal* (Nouvelles acquisitions françaises, nos. 10305-6) and the preparatory dossiers (Nouvelles acquisitions françaises, nos. 10307-8). The excellent notes and critical studies in this edition are by Henri Mitterand. The recently finished 15 volumes of *Œuvres complètes*, with text established by Henri Mitterand and published under the imprint Cercle du Livre précieux by Claude Tchou, is the fullest edition of the complete works, and replaces the older Bernouard edition.

The fiftieth anniversary of the death of Zola in 1952 was the signal for a renewed surge of interest in Zola's works which rescued him from the limbo of a Third Republican Pantheon and promoted him as an author meriting full and serious study. The best biography is the somewhat romanced but judicious and eminently readable *Bonjour Monsieur Zola* by Armand Lanoux (Amiot-Dumont, 1954, and Le Livre de poche). Guy Robert, *Emile Zola: Principes et caractères généraux de son œuvre* (Les Belles-Lettres, 1952) gives an excellent picture of the broad sweep of Zola's work, as does F. W. J. Hemmings, *Emile Zola* (Oxford, Clarendon Press, 1953). The latter, somewhat rewritten and published in a second edition in 1966, is the major work on Zola in English. Angus Wilson's *Emile Zola: An Introductory Study of His Novels* (Secker and Warburg, 1952) is an illuminating essay written from a broadly

Freudian standpoint, though Jean Borie's *Zola et les mythes, ou de la nausée au salut* (Editions du Seuil, 1971) has pressed the matter further and more systematically in a series of brilliant studies. J. H. Matthews, *Les deux Zola* (Droz, 1957) examines the subjective and the objective in Zola. J. C. Lapp's *Zola before the Rougon-Macquart* (University of Toronto Press, 1964) provides a penetrating study of the early Zola, with important suggestions for the study of the mature work. Henri Guillemin's *Présentation des Rougon-Macquart* (Gallimard, 1964) is a series of interesting and somewhat polemical essays on each of the Rougon-Macquart novels.

The most complete bibliography of works (up to 1968) on or closely connected with *Germinal* in particular is given in the Pléiade edition mentioned above, vol. III, 1868–81. Three books deal particularly well with the use of sources in *Germinal*: I.-M. Frandon, *Autour de* Germinal: *la mine et les mineurs* (Droz, 1955); R. H. Zakarian, *Zola's 'Germinal': A Critical Study of its Primary Sources* (Droz, 1972); and E. M. Grant, *Zola's 'Germinal': A Critical and Historical Study* (Leicester University Press, 2nd impression, 1970). The last provides the best overall picture of this aspect, though in less detail than the other two partial studies, and reproduces in full the *Ebauche* of *Germinal*. No book has been devoted completely to a study of what can broadly be called the creative aspect in *Germinal*. The best general essay is M. Girard, 'L'univers de *Germinal*', *Revue des sciences humaines* (1953), 59–76. It is also worth consulting P. Walker, 'Zola's use of color imagery in *Germinal*', *P.M.L.A.* (1962), 442–9; and also his 'Zola's art of characterization in *Germinal*', *L'Esprit créateur* (1964), 60–67.

A good number of interesting and important studies on *Germinal* are to be found in *Les Cahiers naturalistes*, published by the Société littéraire des amis d'Emile Zola and Editeurs Fasquelle (1955–), a review edited currently by Henri Mitterand and dedicated in very large part to the study of Zola. The review *Europe* devoted a special number to Zola in April–May 1968 and contains several very good essays, as does the special number of *Yale French Studies* (42, June 1969), which concentrates particularly on techniques, images and themes in Zola.

Finally, two good surveys of Zola criticism: *Les Critiques de notre temps et Zola* presented by Colette Becker (Garnier, 1972), which concentrates on selected passages of criticism, and the fuller A. Dezalay, *Lectures de Zola* (Colin, 1973), which concentrates more on an analytical account of various types of criticism of Zola's works from the nineteenth century to the present day.